Lessons With Matt

An inspiring story of success strategies
for teachers and parents of tweens and teens

Nick Ambrosino

Also by Nick Ambrosino

Coffee With Ray

Lessons With Matt

An inspiring story of success strategies
for teachers and parents of tweens and teens

Nick Ambrosino

http://www.lessonswithmatt.com

ISBN 13: 978-1502881588

ISBN 10: 1502881586

ABOUT THE AUTHOR

Since 1986, Nick Ambrosino has been a leading expert in the field of human potential and excellence—helping teachers, parents, and students of all ages. He started his career as a public school music teacher and then launched his own private education company in 1988.

Nick is a renowned learning specialist, coach, and speaker for his work with thousands of students, teachers, and parents on creating explosive growth in accountability, productivity, and self-esteem.

What most parents and teachers don't know is how, without resentment or manipulation, to facilitate kids into becoming self-motivated, accountable people, fully capable of setting and achieving their goals.

Teachers turn to Nick to learn how to become master motivators who facilitate their students to new levels of achievement, while reigniting their passion as professional educators and gaining a renewed sense of fulfillment.

Parents seek him out to learn how to communicate in a way that raises confident, self-assured children with high levels of self-esteem.

Nick is available for speaking engagements,
private coaching, or group coaching at

lwm@musicsimplymusic.com

Fax 631 590 5064

DEDICATION

This book is dedicated to all my readers who read *Coffee With Ray* and encouraged me to write the sequel. Thank you! Your enthusiastic response to *Coffee With Ray* was the ignition that lit the fire that fueled *Lessons With Matt*. My wish is that you find *Lessons With Matt* to be a worthy sequel.

ACKNOWLEDGEMENTS

Once again, I thank Angela Canino, my writing muse, who challenged, encouraged, and questioned me, all at the right time and with the right amount of "nudge." Thank you with all of my heart.

Thank you to my dearest friend, Keith, for being my historian. He knew *Coffee With Ray*, better than I. When I wasn't sure if something was presented in *Coffee With Ray*, instead of having to reread it, I just called Keith. Thank you, my friend, for saving me time and energy but, more importantly, thank you for your invaluable friendship. I will forever cherish you and our relationship.

Thank you to my son, Nicholas. He was the first twelve-year-old to read *Coffee With Ray* cover to cover and the *only* person to find chronological discrepancies, which he presented to me with the utmost of care for his father's potentially bruised ego. My incredible son, I simply adore everything you are and everything you will become. I love you.

Finally, thank you to my life partner, my inspiration to lighten up, my wonderful wife of twenty-four years, Diane. Your never-ending belief in me is constant encouragement to "stumble forward." As long as I stumble the entire path with you, I will always be fine. I simply adore you.

x

CHAPTER 1

I pulled up to my first student's home and looked at my watch. NOTES: Our lesson was scheduled for 3:00. I was five minutes early. I took a moment to remind myself of the type of student Katie was—*indecisive* and *cautious* were the adjectives that immediately came to mind. I took a second moment to consider what kind of teacher I needed to be in order to most effectively nurture and support her in creating feelings of success for herself—*compassionate* and *clear* were my descriptors.

I knocked on the door and Katie's mom answered. "Katie, it's Matt. Time for your piano lesson," she shouted upstairs to Katie.

"Hi, Matt."

"Hello, Tara. How are you?"

"Harried. The kids are having a play date with some friends and they're all in the back. I've got to cook dinner, take them to religion, run Daniel to soccer practice, then … Katie, where are you?! Matt's HERE!"

Katie came down the stairs "I'm right here," she said timidly.

"What took you so long? I called you twice."

"I was in the bathroom," she replied uncomfortably.

There was a silence, just long enough to create a vacuum of awkwardness that demanded to be filled. I filled it.

"Hi, Katie. Good to see you. Ready for our lesson together? Katie nodded and we moved into the room with the piano.

"So, how are you today?" I asked.

She pursed her lips and shrugged her shoulders.

"Did you learn anything new in school?" I asked in an even quieter tone, to more accurately match her demeanor.

Another shrug of her shoulders and a nervous, "I don't know."

I waited for a moment, slowing myself down both mentally and physically.

"What did you feel proudest about in your piano playing this week?" I asked as I sat down in my chair, matching her physical position.

"I don't know."

It was a predictable response from her. It either meant she hadn't practiced, was afraid of making a decision, or both. It was probably the latter.

Sometimes "fill in the blank" questions can be overwhelming for a student who hasn't yet built up her decision-making "muscles." I made it more manageable for her by offering a multiple-choice question.

"Well, you have four things in your weekly goal book. Are you proud of how you learned your scales, your note reading, your pop song, or the classical tune?"

"I don't know."

What do you want, Matt? I want this student to start becoming comfortable making a decision or at least be less afraid of doing so. Maybe there were too many choices.

"Okay, between your scales and your pop tune, which do you feel better about?"

"I don't know."

What do you want, Matt? I want this ten-year-old student to start gaining the confidence in her ability to make a decision. Okay, move to yes or no questions.

"Do you feel proud of how you played your pop song?"

Waiting, waiting ….

"I guess so."

Bingo! I'll register that as a success. Albeit small, this was a success! Four weeks ago it took us fifteen minutes to get to this point. We just did it in three.

Sometimes the rewards in my job are measured in microns. But a whole bunch of microns over a longer period of time equates to a significantly larger change. It's like beach glass; water has to gently run over it for a long period of time before it becomes smooth. It doesn't happen overnight. For me, education is a marathon, not a sprint.

My niece had taught me the decision-making lesson five years ago.

My parents had taken our entire family to Disney World for a week-long vacation. At the time, my niece, Renee, was four years old.

Trying to be the cool uncle, I took her and her older sister, Nicole, into Delectable Delights, a candy shop in Downtown Disney. I was going to let them choose whatever single candy they wanted.

Delectable Delights is a palace of candy. For two floors, everywhere you look, candy! My two nieces were like, well they *were*, kids in a candy shop!

The older of the two looked around and within ten minutes had decided she wanted a multicolored striped braid of hard candy that was about one foot long.

While Nicole gleefully chose and started to consume her candy, Renee stood in utter bewilderment at the vastness of this store and the almost infinite variety of candy to choose from. As I watched her, I could see the cogs in her mind seize up and overheat, smoke coming out of her ears. The look in her eyes was one of intimidation and panic.

I stooped down to help her, yet each question was met by a blank stare. It felt like I was watching the hourglass on my computer just spin and spin and spin as it unsuccessfully searched for a file I had requested.

After getting a continued empty response, I took her hand and attempted to lead her out of the store to regroup. She wouldn't budge. She just stood there, a blank-faced statue, as her mental hourglass continued to spin.

Not quite knowing what else to do, I picked her up, at which time she began to scream. Well, screaming is an understatement. She was thrashing her arms and legs in vehement resistance. If my sister-in-law hadn't intervened in the physical struggle, everyone would have assumed I was trying to kidnap the child!

We went outside the store and sat down at a nearby fountain to calm her down. Renee's screams had turned to sobs. My brother, sister-in-law, and I attempted to console her and let her know that we would go back in the store to get her candy.

Since I had brought on the problem, my brother let me find my way out of the hole I had dug.

"You work with kids, Mr. Educator. She's all yours," my brother said as he walked away with his oldest gaily pirouetting by his side. My sister-in-law had a little more compassion and stood within ear shot should I need an assist.

The challenge had been issued, and I was not about to back down.

After Renee had calmed, I looked at her, recognizing my error and said, "That was a lot of candy to choose from."

In between the short gasps and sniffles, she nodded her head. "I want," sniffle, gasp, "my," gasp "candy."

"I understand and we will go back and get you some," I replied. "What kind of candy do you want, chocolate or hard?" I asked.

"Not" sniffle "chocolate," she replied.

"Okay, hard candy. That's a good idea; chocolate melts quickly in this heat. Do you want something with a stick?" I asked, narrowing our choices.

She thought and nodded her head. Excellent, we're in lollipop land.

"What color is your favor ...." *No good. Open-ended question. Almost stepped into the decision-making abyss again. Rephrase.*

"Would you like red, green, yellow, or blue?" I asked, more focused.

"Pink," she countered.

"Great! Pink is awesome; it matches your dress!" I said with enthusiasm, feeling us moving closer to the finish line.

She let me know we were on the right path, by giving me a little smile while smoothing out the front of her dress.

"So, how about we go back in and go to the pink lollipop section?" I asked.

She nodded.

We proceeded, hand in hand, back into Delectable Delights, blinders on, directly to the lollipop section. We did not pass Go; we did not collect $200.

I got lucky. When we got to the pink lollipops, there were only two choices— big or small. As any child would do, she chose the big one, smiled, unwrapped it, held it to her face, and took the first of many licks.

That night, my brother bought the beers. "Nice job with Renee. You were close to the point of no return with her," he said.

"I know, and I also know you enjoyed watching me squirm through it!" I replied.

"Gotta admit, it *was* fun watching the childless bachelor apply parenting skills but, to be honest with you, I never doubted you."

"Thanks," I replied as I reached for my second Guinness.

People tell me I'm a patient teacher; those closer to me know that patience is not one of my virtues. Patience is something you have to exert when you either don't understand and can't accept a person or when your expectations are larger than a person is ready to deliver.

I understand and accept my students for where they're at in their own personal growth process. I have seen many students over the years—students who were confident in their ability to learn and those who were not—students who have been encouraged by their parents to think for themselves and those who were stifled from doing so. It's usually very easy to spot the latter of the two.

When a ten-year-old has difficulty making simple decisions, it often ties back to how that child was treated when making decisions throughout his or her short life.

"What do you want for dinner?" the parent asks.

"Peanut butter and jelly," the child replies.

"Peanut butter and jelly again! You had that yesterday and the day before. Choose something else," the parent responds.

"But you asked me what I wanted," the child defends.

"Anything but peanut butter and jelly," the parent stands his ground.

"But I want peanut butter and jelly," the child holds firmly.

"NO, you can't have peanut butter and jelly again! You'll have chicken!"

And the first lesson of learning to not follow what you want is instilled—its subconscious message: ignore the feelings from your GUT, your inner GPS, that have been put there to guide you to your own personal happiness.

Well if my decisions are not good enough and my life is the sum of my decisions, then I must not be good enough.

It took a chance meeting with a stranger to remind me of this. He simply asked, "What do you want?"

Sometimes teaching or, more accurately, facilitating is a waiting game. Often, much of the wait occurs in compassionate silence, simply pausing for the learner to be ready to learn. There are times I can catalyze the environment and other times in which I simply have to be comfortable with the wait.

People often confuse waiting with doing nothing. They're not the same concepts. Waiting, for me, is an active *inactivity*. It's a choice, a choice to respect the pace of my student. When you look at a compost pile, on the surface, it appears nothing is happening, but below much is occurring. The breakdown of the compost is creating a fertile soil from which much can be grown.

For a child, the skill of learning how to make decisions needs to start small and, as the child's decision-making muscle strengthens, the decisions can begin to have more weight. If a child is not given the chance to make decisions until later in life, the results can be detrimental! Imagine going to the gym and getting under the bench press for the first time with three hundred pounds on the bar above your head! Yet, that is how many parents "teach" decision-making!

Decision-making is a skill and, like many other things, is ultimately best navigated by asking yourself "What do I want?" It is also best nurtured by starting small and working up to the larger potentially life-altering choices.

If a student cannot make a fill-in-the-blank decision, I lighten the load to a multiple-choice decision. Sometimes questions like "What do you want to start with?" can be too open ended for a student who has not yet flexed his decision-making muscles. In this case, I simply ask, "Would you prefer to do x, y, or z?" If the decision-making muscles still cannot bear the load of this weight, I lighten the load again, "Would you like to do x or y?" If it's still too much strain, I ask, "Is it okay if we do x?" And if it's *still* too difficult for the student, I then ask, "Would it be okay with you if, just for today, I decided what we started with?"

It's a process and a lesson in creating challenges that are "just right." Like Ray said, *Goldilocks and the Three Bears* was not just a fairy tale, it was an invaluable piece of educational philosophy disguised as a child's story.

Ray and I had met at Jo's Café back in January. The last time I had actually seen him was in early March. My final communication from him was when Camille, the manager of the café, gave me a letter he had written to me.

The letter, as well as the time I had spent with Ray, had changed my life. Both were auspicious gifts. When I met him, I was ready to quit being a piano teacher and was instead considering a new career as a pizza maker! Pizza making seemed infinitely simpler than trying to teach human beings! My interactions with Ray had validated my choice of career in a way that no degree from any college could have or did. He truly was a gift.

As mysteriously as he had appeared in my life, like the air bubbles of a scuba diver's life-support system disappearing at the surface of the ocean, he had also disappeared. I hadn't heard from him, he hadn't answered his phone, and no one was ever at his home, not even his dog Elvis. Yet his lawn was cut, and the mail didn't pile up. I know because, even though it was out of my way, I occasionally passed by hoping he'd show up. So far, he hadn't.

Odder though, he also hadn't shown up at Jo's Cafe, which he had built as a memorial to his wife who had passed away from breast cancer.

When I first met Ray, it appeared he was a permanent fixture at Jo's, occupying the table for four in the back. Ray's wife, Josephine, was a beloved high school teacher, and Ray had built Jo's Café so students would have a safe place to gather, exchange ideas, and socialize. Not only had Ray built it, but he had also remained its owner.

When I received Ray's letter I was touched, upset, saddened, and inspired. Over the past four months, I had reread it hundreds of times. While my life was full and I felt successful, something was missing … Ray.

My roster of piano students was maxed out. And, even in spite of raising my rates, I had a waiting list of students. Waiting lists were wonderful for my ego, but not beneficial to my bank account. I decided to interview teachers and ended up hiring my first teacher, Diane. My waiting list was quickly converted into paying clients. In one simple decision, I had become someone's boss.

LESSONS WITH MATT

Truth be told, I wasn't quite sure what to do as her boss. I really wasn't comfortable with the title of boss. Though, in more ways than one, I was lucky. Not only were Diane's students thrilled to be working with her, she was also very attractive, and our business relationship had developed into a bit of a romance. I know the old saying, "Don't mix business with pleasure," but matters of the heart are very difficult to negotiate with the brain. So far, my heart was winning, much to the delight of my brain!

I had shifted my regular cycling workouts to running. Running was simpler. A good pair of shoes, shorts, a shirt, and a watch and I was on my way. I could do it anywhere without any special equipment. It took up much less time and, as busy as I was becoming, every moment was valuable.

I was up to three miles in less than thirty minutes. Nine-and-a-half-minute miles were nothing to brag about, but for me it was an accomplishment, so I felt good. The combination of running and changing my eating habits had yielded a weight loss of seven pounds and a feeling of pride.

I was feeling so good about my running that I allowed Diane to talk me into entering my first organized 10K race two Saturdays after Labor Day, just five weeks away.

The race was the world famous Cow Harbor Run. It was renown both because of the beauty of running along the quaint north shore as well as for the spirit-breaking steep climb at mile two, dubbed by the runners as "Widow Hill." Most amateur runners simply walked up the hill to avoid completely burning themselves out.

While the most I had ever run was three miles, I welcomed the challenge of running a 10k, which was a little more than double my present longest distance. I had plenty of time to train and having a goal that was outside of my comfort zone felt good; it motivated me to stay on course with my training.

Ray believed the only way to truly build self-esteem was to continuously stretch our comfort zones by taking on tasks or goals that were a little bit scary, things that pitted us up against what we believed was the limit to our ability. Running a 10K was such a challenge for me.

Diane had been running for most of her life, and it had become a part of her being. She was a much faster runner than I was but, occasionally, on her rest days, we would run together.

In addition to becoming a runner, I had also started taking jazz piano lessons with a new teacher, and I was beginning to regain my love for the instrument.

The lessons were contributing to my feeling of wholeness as a musician. Come to think of it, I was finally feeling whole as a person. Upon reflection, I realized much of this had started around the time I had met Ray, eight months earlier.

Since Ray's disappearance, I had passed by Jo's on a semi-regular basis. In late June however, Jo's closed for two weeks. When I returned in July, it had changed to a Starbucks; the one corner of the earth without a Starbucks was no more! I went in for a cup of coffee to find, as I sadly expected, all the décor had been changed. The canoe hanging from the ceiling was gone, the crossed oars and the life preserver with a breast cancer ribbon above the counter were gone and, even worse, so was Camille, Ray and Jo's long-time friend. I felt depressed and lost; the fragile threads of webbing linking me to Ray were breaking one by one.

I started to wonder if Ray had just been a figment of my imagination. Did I really meet with such an inspiring man, or was it a dream? In my disillusioned state, had my mind created a being to save me? If that was true, then I wouldn't have the letter he wrote me, and I did.

I reached into my jacket pocket and removed the tattered letter that, on a daily basis for the past six months, I had read and reread—the letter that, after continued reading, had slowly but assuredly reshaped the way I thought—the letter that provided sanity and inspiration to me when I inevitably had those frustrating and discouraging moments as a teacher.

I carefully removed it from the envelope addressed in Ray's handwriting. The envelope simply read "Matt." I gently opened and unfolded it from the quarter folds that made it fit in my breast pocket and reread it for the ten thousandth time:

My Dear Friend,

While you may see yourself as a teacher of a subject, music, you are so much more! You are a teacher of people; that is your true specialization, not just the subject of music. Yes, when students come to you they want to learn a special set of skills but, as an imperative compliment to that specific skill set, you teach them how to learn, how to grow! What an incredible gift that is!

Ray's letter continued, but the end had always left me with an uncomfortable feeling.

We will meet again when the time is right for both of us. Thank you for the gift of your friendship. I am privileged to have had the opportunity to share ideas with such an open-minded student, as well as to have learned from you. You will thrive and, as a result, so will your students.

Yes, you taught me too. No relationship is one-sided. People do not come into your life for you to either serve them or for them to serve you. Both parties are served by the relationship, both have gifts to unwrap and give through the relationship ....

Your friend,

Ray

CHAPTER 2

After five weeks of hardcore training, I was excited about running my first organized race, so much so that I didn't sleep well the night before. After speaking with other runners at the Cow Harbor Run, this appeared to be a common occurrence.

NOTES:

The air was crisp, a prelude to what each fall day was going to be once fall officially arrived. It was a bit odd to have this cooler weather so early in September; usually, we were experiencing an Indian summer. Because of the cooler weather, many runners brought "throw-a-ways" with them. Throw-a-ways were an extra layer of clothing that runners wore for warmth at the beginning of the race but which were removed and discarded on the sidelines, with the understanding that they would probably not get them back. A throw-a-way was usually an old sweatshirt or t-shirt that you were going to discard anyhow.

I didn't bring a throw-a-way, so I was cold while waiting in my wave at the starting line of the race. Since I had submitted a nine-minute mile as my goal, I was put in the ninth wave, meaning that my group of runners would go off as the ninth group. My goal was to finish in under an hour.

The faster runners always started the race first, so as not to be held up by those of us who were slower. Diane was in the sixth wave, with a goal of finishing under forty-five minutes.

My wave had approximately 600 runners. The entire race had over 5,000 participants. As there was a cash prize for the first place runner and a $5,000 bonus to the runner who broke the course record, the Cow Harbor Run drew athletes from throughout the United States. The present course record was set in 2011 with a time of 28 minutes and 17 seconds! The five lead runners in this year's run, two of whom were Olympic hopefuls, had each logged previous times of under 29 minutes!

There was also a $500 prize for the winner of the Masters category, which was for women and men over the age of 40. While there wasn't a cash prize for each age bracket, the top three finishers were awarded medals.

This year's race was a bit different because the American Breast Cancer Association was also sponsoring it. One of the original founders of the race had recently died after a long bout with breast cancer. In tribute, many of the runners wore the pink breast cancer ribbon on their jerseys. Ten percent of the proceeds from the run were being given to the American Breast Cancer Association.

One of the lead runners was a woman who was competitive enough to have a chance at breaking the women's record of 32 minutes and 26 seconds. If she was successful, she would also receive a $5,000 bonus, half of which she planned on donating to the American Breast Cancer Association, in honor of her mother who had died of breast cancer five years earlier.

Diane and I arrived by car to the race location at 6:30 AM. We parked in the lot of a nearby restaurant a half-mile from the race starting line. We wished each other luck (more her to me!) and then reported to our designated areas. My wave was supposed to start at 7:39, nine minutes after the first wave began.

The race was well organized. I picked up my race bag containing promotional items from various sports retailers—a water bottle, some energy products, and a headband. We were also given a microchip that clipped onto our running shoes. The microchip logged our time as we crossed the finish line. I guess, with $5,000 on the line, accuracy was very important for the people in the first wave! For me, I hope it logged the DAY I finished and had a GPS tracking device to find me in case I didn't!

I jogged back to my car to deposit my souvenirs and then returned to the starting line, making a pit stop, along with hundreds of other runners, at one of the forty outdoor temporary bathrooms.

At exactly 7:20 AM, the race organizers came on the PA system and welcomed the appropriate dignitaries (this was an election year for the local town positions, so people were politicking). Since a local television station was broadcasting the race, a helicopter hovered above. A local nine-year-old guitarist named Cole performed the Jimmy Hendrix version of the national anthem. He was simply amazing! The musician in me was impressed by his prowess; the music teacher in me wanted to congratulate both him and his guitar teacher. There was a moment of silence for Margaret Avenir, the race founder who had recently passed away. A digital countdown over the starting line began descending from ten. When the clock hit zero, a starter's gun was fired and the first wave went off. Each minute, thereafter, a new wave started. I started my race at exactly 7:39 AM.

Throughout the first half mile, I had butterflies in my stomach. I tried to find my pace and someone else in the pack who was running at my speed. Diane had cautioned me to sit back in the pack, as the natural tendency of a new runner was to try to get to the front early in the race. This was not the kind of race that an amateur, running for the first time, could complete with any decency if he started in the front. She told me to find someone who appeared to be at my pace and then to run right behind them. I zoned in on a man a little older than me and let him lead.

There were many types of characters in the Cow Harbor Run. For the most part, people were dressed in standard running gear, but there were a few who were out of the ordinary.

I was passed by a guy in a cow outfit (I figured a cow should be able to outrun me—heck, he had four legs!), a ballerina (lighter on her feet—easier to go faster was my justification as she pirouetted by!), and two kids who couldn't have been older than ten (no justification for them—I was simply in awe as they blew past me, as though I was standing still!).

By the end of the first mile, and just in time for Widow Hill, I had settled into my pace. In an effort to save my legs and lungs for the remaining four miles, I chose to heed Diane's advice and used a brisk walk as my means of scaling this small mountain.

Once Widow Hill was completed, the race was uneventful. The course meandered through neighborhoods that surrounded the harbor. It was difficult but uneventful. At the end of mile four, all of that changed. It just became difficult. My legs and lungs started screaming for me to stop. Bubbles of spit were leaking from my mouth like speech balloons yelling the word "HELP!"

I reached for a cup of water that a local homeowner had placed on a folding table outside of his home. As I jostled it to my mouth, I drank what was left, crushed the cup, and threw it on the side of the road. While I was drinking, my mind was focused on something else, so I didn't feel the pain. Once I finished the water, my legs reminded my mind that they wanted to stop and the pain increased. I was officially in an internal battle—mind versus body.

I was ready to quit and admit defeat when I heard Ray's mantra in my head, "What do you want?" The first time I had heard that was when I was in his home, and he was serving me coffee. I thought he was asking me what I wanted in my coffee. He wasn't. He was asking me what I wanted in my career and in my life. Up until that point in my life, I had never really considered answering that question and the words that came out of my mouth had caught me off guard.

He had continuously reminded me, "Focus on what you want." Right now, that seemed like sage advice. Hmm, what did I want? I wanted the race to end. That was correct, but not one hundred percent accurate. I liked running the race; what I didn't like was the pain. I wanted the pain to stop. That was true, but I realized I wanted something else more than for the pain to stop. I wanted to prove to myself that I could accomplish what I put my mind to. Yes, that's what I wanted.

When I focused on the pain, I just felt frustrated with myself. So, instead, I changed my thinking and started to mentally review my conversations with Ray about frustration and the story of *Goldilocks and the Three Bears*. When we spoke about it back in February, it was in reference to assisting my students in feeling successful. The Three Bears story was a way for a student to gauge a challenge so that he was always feeling successful. Was this task too big, too small, or just right? I had applied it to my students and now it was time to practice what I preached.

The task was a 10K. I didn't have control over that! What did I have control over? My pace! Was my pace too fast, too slow, or just right? I immediately recognized that it was too fast. I slowed down a bit to accommodate my ability (or lack thereof!) and the vocal outbursts from my legs and lungs eased.

What did I want? I wanted to finish this race. But it was almost two more miles! I looked ahead and, about four telephone poles away, I saw a blue mailbox. I could run to that. That was my next goal.

As I reached the mailbox, I started to hear the Rocky theme. I was now officially hallucinating! But the hallucination persisted. I saw a runner ahead of me raise his arms in the Rocky pose and considered that other people might be hearing it as well. The runner next to me shadow boxed, and I decided that either EVERYONE was hallucinating the same thing simultaneously or maybe someone was actually playing the song! Since I still heard the music, I deduced that I had not yet lost my sanity and made the house with the blaring music my next "finish line."

As I approached the Rocky house, I too put my hands up above my head, mimicking Rocky Balboa's position at the top of the stairs in Philadelphia. The crowd started cheering for me. That was exactly what I needed to get to the finish line. My adrenaline kicked in and the focus on the fun as well as my small successes made running easier or at least more tolerable.

There was one final hill at the beginning of mile six. While it wasn't as steep or as long as Widow Hill on James Street, I was much more tired than I had been at mile two, but the cheering of the crowd literally made it feel like someone was behind me pushing me up the climb.

The final descent toward the finish line provided a picturesque view of a quaint north shore town lined with local shops and cheering spectators. It reminded me of a Norman Rockwell painting.

As I was propelled down the hill by the fuel of the cheering crowd, I could hear the announcer calling off the names of many of the runners. I'm not sure if he said my name, because I was too overwhelmed with the supportive energy of the crowd and my own personal feeling of success. As I crossed the finish line, I could hear my brain celebrate! Fireworks erupted in my mind's eye. I had won—certainly not the race, but my own personal battle. I was ecstatic!

Ray would've told me the feeling I had was that of growth. I had accomplished something outside of my comfort zone and had grown as a person. Really, that's what growth was; it was the expansion of your comfort zone. The effort to do this was usually uncomfortable and sometimes downright painful, but the reward was an increase in self-esteem. The reward was, as I told my students, the feeling of pride!

As I walked to release the tension and fatigue in my legs, I saw Diane fifty yards from the finish line. She was facing me, speaking with someone, and looked well recovered, most likely having arrived about fifteen minutes earlier. When she saw me approaching, she ran to me, and gave me a celebratory hug.

"You finished! I'm so proud of you! How do you feel?"

"Yep, I finished! I'm physically spent, but mentally and emotionally I'm charged!" I replied.

"I'm so excited for you!" she said and gave me another hug, this time accompanied by a kiss.

"I was just talking to one of the top three finishers in the men's 70-79 division. He was in your wave and came in at exactly 54 minutes, which is an 8-minute-42-second mile—quite an impressive time for his age!

"If I saw your time correctly, you finished in just over 59 minutes."

When I handed in my microchip, the young woman manning the station told me that my exact time was 59 minutes and 2.1 seconds. I had run 9-minute-31-second miles. It was not quite as impressive as someone forty plus years my senior running a full one minute per mile faster than me but, for my first race, I was proud!

The weather had warmed and people were celebrating their personal victories. Families were reuniting, and proud young children were running into the arms of their mothers and fathers who had run. A local five-piece southern rock band had started playing "Life in the Fast Lane" by the Eagles. For the next hour, runners continued to cross the finish line. The last person to finish was a ninety-two-year-old woman who had taken up running at the tender age of eighty-five! Her finishing time was 1 hour and 56 minutes, but the cheering that accompanied her made it sound like she was the first person to cross the line!

After this inspiring woman had completed the race, there was an announcement for all runners to go to the gazebo so the medals could be distributed. I was having my third beer and half-heartedly walked over with Diane. I was ready to leave, but Diane wanted to stay to see if the woman who was slated to break the women's course record had accomplished her goal and won the $5,000.

I was standing roughly sixty yards from the gazebo, surrounded by what felt like ten thousand people. The first awards distributed were to the winners of the over 90 category. All three runners who had entered this category medaled ... simply because they were the only competitors in the category!

Next, they called up the gold, silver, and bronze winners of the men and women's 80-89 year-old category. When the man who had won the men's category accepted his medal and came up to the podium, the crowd went crazy! Apparently, he had won every age category he had entered since he started running the race, at the age of 63, twenty years ago!

The next group was the 70-79 Masters category. The winners of the women's division were announced first. The crowd applauded politely as each recipient stepped up to the podium to accept her medal. Next, they announced the men's winners. "John Kefa, Ray Mandino, Emmanuel Thomas."

I casually took a sip of my beer and then turned to look at the podium. I started coughing, as I choked on my beverage. *Ray Mandino? RAY?!* I looked again in disbelief. Diane, noticing, asked, "Matt, are you okay?"

I gasped for air like I was running the final hill at mile six. There, not sixty yards away, stood Ray! Ray from Jo's! Ray who had disappeared for six months!

I was shocked because, first, I had been trying to get in touch with him since March, and there he was right in front of me and, second, because I had never known his last name! *Mandino*. I started moving forward, completely forgetting about Diane. I needed to get to the podium!

The crowd was thick and my progress was slow. I started feeling anxious as I lost sight of him. The announcer called up the next group of winners, but all I heard was a disjointed fugue orchestrated for announcer, crowd, and southern rock band.

By the time I made it to the podium, Ray was nowhere in sight. *Damn it*! Six months and now just sixty yards had separated me from him. To make matters worse, not only had I not reconnected with Ray, but now I had lost Diane as well.

The glory of my accomplishment was fading quickly. I circled around the podium and looked back into the crowd. I jumped up to get a look above the mass of people! There was nothing, not a single trace. Just as he had so quietly disappeared in March, he had done so once again. What was it going to take to reconnect with him?

I heard someone call my name. It was Diane. "Where did you disappear to? Are you okay?"

"Yes, I'm fine. I'm sorry for just leaving you. It's just that when they announced the silver medal winner in the men's 70-79 category, it was Ray!"

"Ray, as in Jo's Café Ray?" she asked.

Diane had heard countless stories of my interactions with Ray and the impact he had had on my teaching style and my life. Some of the techniques I shared with her about teaching came from my time with Ray. She knew how important he had been to me. I had even shared with her the letter he had written me.

"Yes, that Ray! Ray *Mandino*. I had never known his last name until it was just announced."

"Well, where is he?" she asked sensing my panic.

"I don't know. As I worked my way to the podium, I lost him in the crowd."

She instinctively turned to look for Ray, only to realize she didn't know what he looked like.

"What was he wearing?" she asked.

"He had on a pink shirt. Of course! This race was supported by the American Breast Cancer Society. Ray runs many of those races because his wife died from breast cancer! I should have known."

The fact that Ray was wearing a pink shirt was of no help whatsoever. The American Breast Cancer Society was very well represented at this event; everywhere you looked, there was someone in pink. An aerial photo would've looked like a Van Gogh of pink carnations.

As if on cue, an announcer came on to tell the crowd that the Cow Harbor Run had been extremely successful this year and it was making a $27,000 donation to the American Breast Cancer Society.

With obligatory applause and one last look around, I resigned myself to the fact that there was a slim chance of finding Ray, at least for today. On the bright side, I knew he was around, and I knew his last name, so I could go to his house later today or tomorrow.

Diane and I started walking back to my car. The parking lot was filled with cars from many states—Pennsylvania, New Jersey, Delaware, Massachusetts, Vermont, Virginia—and then suddenly one vanity plate abruptly caught my attention. "COACH." The name on the plate was "COACH." That was Ray's Jeep!

He was still here! I convinced Diane to wait with me by Ray's Jeep. She conceded to my childlike pleading but, after twenty minutes, he had not returned.

"Why don't you leave a note on his windshield?" she asked patiently.

"I'm afraid he won't respond."

"If he's as good a friend as you describe, he'll respond," she said.

I went to my car, about fifteen cars further down in the lot, tore a blank page from a music manuscript book, and composed a note.

Ray,

I was so excited to see you at the race! Congratulations on medaling in your division! I tried to find you when they announced your name. I would love to reconnect and catch up. So much has happened since we last spoke. Please call me as soon as possible.

Your friend,

Matt

I walked back to Ray's car where Diane was still waiting. Dejected, I replaced the pages of advertisements on his windshield with the note I had written.

Diane grabbed my hand and we returned to my car in silence.

CHAPTER 3

I had wanted to pass by Ray's house on Sunday, but my band had a performance that was three hours away. The rest of my week was so packed with teaching and other meetings, that I didn't make the time to visit him until Friday. I had called his home phone several times throughout the week, only to have it just ring. On Friday, I decided to just drive by.

When I arrived, I was surprised; Ray's garage door was open and there he was, working on a canoe. The inside of his garage was an incredible wood shop! While I didn't know much about carpentry equipment, there was a lot of it and he kept the workshop cleaner than an operating room before surgery.

I wanted to run up and give him a hug, question him on where he had been for the past six months, vent my frustration on how he just up and left, and simultaneously thank him for the incredible impact he had made in my life. All I said was, "Hi."

Ray responded with similar casualness, as if a six-month gap hadn't existed, as if I had just seen him yesterday (which was close to accurate, if he had actually known I was at the race!), "Hello, Matt."

"Hi, Ray." I felt the awkwardness of a couple who had once been in love, broke up, and had then accidentally met on the street.

"Great to see you," I responded without making eye contact.

"Would you hand me the plane?"

27

"Excuse me?"

"The plane, the tool next to your right hand on the table."

"Oh, this thing?" I asked.

"Yes, *that* thing," Ray replied.

"What's it for?" I asked, trying to make small talk.

"It's used to cut thin slices from a piece of wood."

To be honest, I really didn't care about cutting wood. What I wanted to know was where he had been. What had happened in his life that motivated him to disappear for the past six months? Why hadn't he called me after the race or when he arrived back in town? His first words of coaching, from six months ago, ran through my head, "What do you want?" What I wanted was clarity and an explanation. I didn't know or care if I was asking for too much, but that's what I wanted. So I cut to the chase.

"Where have you been?"

The question felt abrupt, intrusive, and abrasive, but I didn't know of any other way of asking it. I had gotten much better utilizing direct and effective communication skills with my students, but sometimes I was too direct or not direct enough with my friends, in this case the former.

"Traveling."

"Do you want to expand on that?" I responded abruptly and again, too abrasively.

"Not right now," Ray commented without any obvious emotion.

"Do you want to assist me with this canoe? I could use another hand."

I was passing by on my way back home from lessons. I really wasn't dressed for the occasion and what I really wanted to say was "Not right now," but all that came out was a polite "Sure."

"You can take the sander and start sanding the bow. Just make sure you sand in the direction of the grain in the wood. Don't go against the grain."

"Which end is the bow?"

"The front."

The canoe looked pretty symmetrical to me and to confuse matters more, it was upside down on supports.

"Which end is the front?" I asked.

Ray cracked a smile and pointed to the end at which I was standing. "That end. That's the bow, the front."

I picked up the sander and started sanding, moving the sander back and forth with the grain. About a minute passed by in silence.

"You know it has on 'on' switch? It's a cordless sander," Ray said.

"Now I do!" I replied, embarrassed. I turned it on. "Oh, it works much better this way!"

Ray smiled. "Better or more effectively?"

"Yes, you're correct, oh Great Diamond Distinction Master, more effectively."

Ray just smiled again. His smile was disarming.

I shouted above the hum of the sander, "I saw you at the Cow Harbor Run. I believe you medaled in the Masters category. Congratulations, Mr. Mandino."

"Thank you," Ray shouted back, matter-of-factly.

"I never knew your last name until I heard the announcer say it at the awards ceremony. I don't even know what made me look up. But there you were! Ray Mandino. To say I was surprised was an understatement."

"You never asked," he said without taking his eyes off the canoe.

"Did you get the note I left on your Jeep at the race?" I asked.

"Yes," was his curt reply.

"Is this the canoe from Jo's?"

"Yes."

"Did you sell it?"

"The canoe?" he asked.

"No, Jo's!"

"Yes."

"Why?"

"It was the right time. It helped a lot of people."

"Selling Jo's helped a lot of people?" I queried.

"Yes, Camille, the students who hung out there, and me," he replied.

"Do you mind me asking how it helped all those people?" I asked, confused.

"No, I don't mind. Camille had been at Jo's six days a week since it had opened. To her, it was a way of keeping Jo alive, but it wasn't keeping her relationship with her husband healthy. When I sold it, I gave her a retirement package so that she and her husband could travel and not worry about how they were going to pay for it. The last postcard I got from her was from Spain."

"How did it help the students?"

"I built Jo's on a piece of land I had inherited many years ago. Because of a grandfather clause in the real estate contract, that particular location turned out be a very valuable piece of property. It was the only lot in the area that could sell food. Starbucks offered me a very attractive price for the land and the building. I used some of that money to set up the Josephine Mandino Scholarship Fund to help students who decide to go into education as a career choice. Now Jo's memory lives on past the café.

"All the employees were rewarded with a bonus based upon their years of service."

"Didn't you need some of that money for yourself?" I asked.

"No," Ray replied simply.

I thought for a moment and then turned the sander back on, moving it slowly across the rough surface of the wood, in the direction of the grain. I sanded about a third of the bow before Ray said it was quitting time.

"I'm going to be working on this canoe tomorrow if you want to come back and assist," Ray shared.

"Sure. I'm going out to dinner with my girlfriend in the early evening, but I can come by in the morning, if you're making the coffee," I replied.

"Okay. I have an interesting new blend from my travels. Nine o'clock?"

"See you at nine," I answered.

The entire way home, I was paying attention to the road, but my mind was elsewhere. That one-hour encounter with Ray felt surreal.

CHAPTER 4

Saturday morning I awoke at 7:00 AM and ran three miles. After a shower and a healthy breakfast of yogurt and granola, I hopped into my car around 8:15 and made my way to Ray's. I arrived five minutes before nine to find him in the garage sanding the canoe. It was as though he had continued working on it all night.

"Good morning!" I yelled out to him above the hum of the sander.

"Good morning, Matt!" Ray called back. "Great timing; I'm ready to take a coffee break!"

"Break time? We haven't even started working yet!" I responded.

"Distinction ... *you* haven' started working yet. I've been at this thing since 7:00 AM. It's time for coffee." Ray replied.

"Okay, if you insist," I said.

We went into his kitchen; it looked unchanged from when I had visited him back in March. I only recognized two things that were different.

The first was that Ray wasn't brewing his coffee in the vacuum pot he had previously used and the second was that the mugs he had placed on the counter were from Hawaii and Alaska, not Utah and Texas.

"Hey, Ray, no vacuum pot?"

"When I was traveling, the vacuum pot took up too much room, so I brought a French Press with me. Guess I've just grown accustomed to using it over the past six months. It brews a nice cup of jo," he replied as he gently caressed his wife's wedding band on his left pinkie.

I then noticed that something else was missing—Elvis. "Where's Elvis?" I asked with caution.

"Oh, he's out back. He's lying in the mulch in one of the beds. Let's see if he wants to come in to meet an old friend." Ray opened the back door and gave a quick whistle. Seconds later, Elvis came trotting up the deck.

"Hey, Elvis, long time no see!" I said.

Apparently Elvis immediately remembered me; his tail started keeping a beat against the wall, as he began licking my face. I kneeled down giving him a firm welcoming scratch around his ears.

"Looks like he remembers you," Ray said.

"It appears so." I replied.

Ray poured coffee into the Hawaiian mug. He said he had found the blend at a small roaster in Washington State. I added some cream, being careful not to overfill my mug. I'm glad he had given me the Hawaiian mug because I had always wanted to visit Maui. It was one of the destinations on my bucket list. In addition, the mug from Alaska was squarely shaped with rounded corners. I never quite knew how to drink out of one of those mugs. Do I use the corner as a channel for the liquid, or was I supposed to drink from one of the flat sides?

"Remember the napkin on which you drew the picture of the Comfort Zone?" I asked, reminiscing.

"Yes, I do."

"I still have it! It's a very powerful tool for me when I see a student feeling less than successful," I replied.

"I'm glad my little napkin drawing was valuable to you. Maybe someday it will be worth a lot of money. I heard Picasso was famous for jotting down sketches on napkins that eventually sold for incredible sums," Ray said.

"That would be fantastic! Would I have to split the proceeds with you?" I asked teasingly.

"Nope, just make a donation to the Josephine Mandino Fund," Ray quickly replied.

"Can I assume, based upon these mugs, that you visited Hawaii and Alaska?"

"That would be an accurate assumption," Ray replied.

"Were they two of the places you visited in the past six months?" I asked.

"Yes, but the Hawaiian mug was from a trip Jo and I took years ago.

"Jo had always dreamed of living in Hawaii for a bit, but she died before we had the chance to do so. On this last trip, I brought her ashes with me and, as per her request, scattered them on Mauna Kea, Hawaii's highest peak."

After fifteen minutes, our coffee break ended and we made our way back to the garage to continue working on the canoe. Ray handed me the sander and jokingly asked if I knew how to use it.

"Last night after you left, I finished all of the coarse sanding. This morning, I put a medium-grit sandpaper on the sander. After you finish the medium grit, you can change the sandpaper to a fine grit. It shouldn't take more than twenty minutes on medium before the wood is ready for the fine. If you start on the fine grit too soon, you'll know it because it won't feel like you're getting anywhere with the sanding and the wood will start to heat up."

As I started sanding, the steady hum of the sander acted like a mantra and relaxed my mind. I started to reflect on what Ray had just said.

Sanding, like education, is a process of slow gentle change. If I "forced" the wood to change—become smooth too quickly— the wood would burn from sanding one spot for too long. It was just like if I pushed a student to grow too quickly or with too much attention to very fine-tuned specific details for which he was not ready; he could end up with the heated feeling of frustration. If the sandpaper was too fine, it would take a lot longer to accomplish my task, just as too specific of a task could quickly discourage a learner.

Choosing the appropriate grit sandpaper was like choosing the correct gradient for my student. In addition, it was always best to sand with the grain, in the direction of least resistance, just as it was always best to utilize the path of least resistance with a student. By moving in the direction of the grain, you were not trying to change the natural direction of the wood; you were respecting its unique qualities. While it's certainly necessary for a student to work outside of his comfort zone in order to grow, there is a fine line between healthy, motivating stress and the distress of too much resistance. Too much resistance means the wood cannot, or is not yet ready, to be changed that much. The art of teaching is about walking this fine line.

When I turned off my sander to change the sandpaper, I shared what I was thinking with Ray. He smiled and acknowledged my realization.

"Yes, when you sand, you move from a *general* large-grit sandpaper, to an increasingly *more specific* fine-grit paper. Just as when you learn, as your proficiency grows, you move from general knowledge to an increasingly more specific knowledge. As the wood's "proficiency" grows and it becomes smoother, we change the fineness of the sandpaper. That's exactly what you would do with a student. And, like I said yesterday, you always want to go in the direction of the grain, otherwise you can ruin the wood. As much as you can, take the path of least resistance."

Ray and I worked for a couple of hours more. When I left him to get ready for my date with Diane, I put a piece of sandpaper in my pocket.

CHAPTER 5

After Ray's, I headed home to do some house cleaning and handle a bit of business. Tonight, Diane and I were going to dinner at a restaurant in Venetian Shores. I was going to pick her up at 5:00 PM.

NOTES:

Venetian Shores was an interesting town. The developer who had created it loved Venice (another place on my bucket list to visit) and had built a community interspersed with small lakes connected by white bridges. No two houses were the same. There were Victorian mansions, French villas, Spanish Tudors, and expansive ranches. In the winter, when kids were ice-skating and playing hockey on the lakes, it was as though you were looking into a Norman Rockwell painting. In the summer, you could find children and adults fishing and canoeing.

Venetian Shores had become a popular town for my music services. It appeared that when one person in the area discovered a service they liked, they shared it with all of their friends. They all used the same doctor, dentist, orthodontist, private school, plumber, electrician, and, much to my benefit, private music teacher.

To top matters off, one of my student's had an uncle who opened a restaurant that Diane and I enjoyed. Tonight, we were headed there for dinner and drinks.

When we arrived, I found a spot near the front and parked the car.

As always, Diane looked beautiful. Her skin was tan and she wore a form-fitting white top that showed off her stunning figure as well as the definition in her arms, of which she was very proud. She had a flowing print skirt and sensible, stylish shoes she had bought on a trip to Italy.

We sat at the bar for a drink. She ordered a Side Car and I ordered an Old-Fashioned. According to the bartender, Heather, drinks from the Great Gatsby era were once again becoming popular, so our choices were not a surprise to her. She said she actually preferred making drinks that required a bit of skill as opposed to just pouring a beer.

"Guess who I met yesterday?" I asked Diane.

"Hmmm … Ray?" She answered quickly.

"How did you know?" I replied, disappointed that I didn't get to share the news.

"Oh, I don't know, I guess it's just a woman's intuition."

"Last night on my way home from teaching, I decided to pass by his house. He was working in his garage on his canoe. We spoke and I went back this morning to help him."

"How is he?" Diane asked.

"He looks like the exact same Ray I knew at the beginning of the year."

"Did he tell you where he went?"

"No, he didn't offer too much information, although I did find out that two of his stops were Alaska and Hawaii."

"Wow, the most northern and southern parts of the United States," Diane replied.

"Hmm, I didn't realize that when he said it. His trip to Hawaii sounded like it was difficult," I continued.

"Why was that?" Diane asked.

"He said he spread his wife's ashes on Mauna Kea, Hawaii's highest peak."

"Wow, I didn't expect that," Diane replied.

"You didn't expect him to spread his wife's ashes in Hawaii? Why would you?" I asked confused by her comment.

"No, I didn't expect that he didn't share anything with you about where he was for six months. You said he was your friend."

"He is," I said defensively.

"Then why did he not offer an explanation?"

"I don't know," I replied.

"Did you ask for one?" Diane asked.

"Yes, but most of his responses were short. So I didn't push any further. Well, actually, I wanted to when I arrived at his house. I had all sorts of thoughts running through my head, but all that came out when I saw him was, 'Hi'."

"Sounds like you were a little star struck," Diane said.

I was starting to feel like I was under attack, and I was beginning to feel annoyed. "No. I asked him where he had been for the past six months and he told me he had been traveling. Then I asked him if he wanted to expand on that and he replied, 'Not right now.' So I respected his choice and just let it be. What are you trying to get at?" I asked, the pitch of my voice rising.

"You said you and Ray were friends. Friends keep in touch; friends return phone calls; friends text."

"Ray doesn't know how to text. He doesn't even have a cell phone. Heck he still writes his thoughts in a small book he calls an 'iPad' which stands for his Idea Pad," I replied.

"That's what I mean. You're getting too caught up in the words. It's not about how he keeps in touch. To me it's odd that he *didn't* keep in touch, especially after the letter he wrote to you," Diane continued.

"Maybe he just needed some time alone," I stated.

"Really Matt? Six months? No goodbye? No contact? I mean, at the race, you left him a note on his car, and he didn't even have the common courtesy to call. He closed his café without a word. Don't you find that odd? I'd be surprised if he closed it while traveling. He either knew he was going to close it before he left and had all the paper work in order, or he was in town and closed it. Considering how special Jo's was to you, don't you find it a bit circumspect that he would do so without even mentioning it to you? It sounds like you're defending him, trying to find a reason for it to be okay for him to have left your relationship on hold," she pushed back.

The hostess interrupted our conversation to let us know our table was ready.

We sat down and ordered the tasting menu with a wine pairing. For the most part, our meal was eaten in silence, as Diane's comments were running through my mind and gut. I don't really remember tasting any of the food and, to pour more salt on the wound, it appeared that Diane loved and fully enjoyed her meal. Mine just tasted like resentment.

Our server came over several times to make sure everything was to our satisfaction, and each time I replied with a very dismissive, "It's fine, thank you." After the plates from our last course were removed, she asked us if we wanted dessert. I declined and I could see from the look in Diane's eye that she knew I just wanted to get home.

When we walked to the car, I walked over to driver's side and slid into the seat. Diane stood outside the passenger door, waiting for me to open it for her. I'm usually a gentleman and do so before entering the car myself. This time I just reached across from the inside and pulled the lever while pushing the door open.

Diane got in the car and looked at me with raised eyebrows.

"You seem upset," she stated.

"No," I replied curtly.

"Matt, if you're upset, 'fess up to your feelings. Please don't pretend that nothing's bothering you. We ate our entire meal at one of our favorite restaurants in silence. If that doesn't say something is wrong, what does?"

"Okay, I'm upset! You have no right attacking Ray or me that way! You don't even know him! He's very important to me. He helped me get back on path with my teaching and with my life. There, I said it!"

"I get that but, in my opinion, that doesn't give him the right to handle your friendship with irresponsibility, which to me is what he did. And because you hold him in such high esteem, you let him. If you're angry, please be clear as to whom you're angry with. Is it really me or are you just displacing your anger towards Ray at me? You said it yourself; you didn't say what you wanted to say when you saw him, you just sort of, and I don't mean any disrespect, but you just sort of rolled over submissively and said 'Hi.' To paraphrase Ray's words, is that what you want?" Diane replied.

Wow, did she let me have it! I still felt angry, yet, as painful as it was to hear, I knew in my heart she was right. I was out of integrity with myself.

"No, it's not what I want," I replied humbly.

"Then you have a responsibility to call him on his alleged irresponsibility. Wasn't it Ray who told you that relationships are one hundred percent and one hundred percent, not fifty-fifty?"

"Yep, it was," I replied.

"Then both he and you should practice what you preach, and it seems like it will have to start with you," she replied.

"What if it breaks the relationship?" I asked.

"Matt, you can't have a breakthrough to the next level of anything in life without first having a bit of a breakdown. I think that breakdowns are like naturally created forest fires. The pine trees need the heat to explode their pinecones to reseed the forest. In the short term, a breakdown appears to be ugly but, in the long run, it's actually a gift, a breakthrough, a rebirth," she replied.

"Then I guess you could call what we just went through as a bit of a breakthrough. Right?" I asked.

"Yes," was her simple reply.

CHAPTER 6

I spent all of Sunday thinking about what Diane had said. The more I considered it, the more annoyed I got, not at Diane, but at myself. By Sunday evening, I was so consumed by her words that I made a decision to call Ray the next morning.

NOTES:

On Monday morning, just after I had my morning coffee, I dialed his number, fully expecting (perhaps even hoping!) that it would just ring. When he actually picked up the phone, I was momentarily caught off guard and speechless. My knee-jerk reaction was to lace my words with a touch of sarcasm.

"Wow, so you actually do answer your phone."

By his response, it was clear he knew it was me. It even appeared he might have been expecting my call.

"I deserved that," Ray replied. "Would you like to get together and talk?"

"How about tomorrow? Do you know where Byldenburgh Park is?"

"Yes. That will be fine. Will ten o'clock work for you?"

"Yes, see you then."

I hung up and just stared at the phone. As freeing as that call was, it was also scary knowing I was committed to speaking my mind. I guess I could call that emotional growth because it was simultaneously intimidating and inviting. I felt empowered.

On Tuesday morning, I completed my morning routine of a cup of cappuccino and a three-mile run, in that order. Fall was just beginning to show its colors and the air was crisp. I was glad I had decided to run this morning as it got rid of some of the adrenaline I was feeling in anticipation of my meeting with Ray.

As much as I liked clarity and openness in my relationships, I wasn't always comfortable with the initiation of those types of conversations. It took a good bit of courage to just make the phone call to Ray and even more to meet with him.

While I was readily aware that I was an adult, I was, as I once read in one of those self-help books, still a "human becoming." Part of my becoming was navigating through childhood conditioning patterns that were ineffective for me as an adult.

One of those patterns was the "respect for your elders and authority figures" that was instilled in me by my parents. The extension of respect I had been taught had nothing to do with knowledge, wisdom, or the rightful earning of it but, instead, was simply to do with age or level of social hierarchy.

Obviously, as an adult, this axiom had little validity and many flaws. One of those flaws was the uncomfortable feeling I got when I questioned an elder or authority figure. My meeting with Ray brought some of this up, but I clearly saw the axiom's ineffectiveness in my life, so I had made a conscious decision to stretch my comfort zone and take it on.

Blydenburgh Park was a county-run park with several large fields that could be rented for events (usually for family reunions and summer picnics), a pond on which you could fish and/or take out a boat, and many trails that meandered through the wooded area. There was also a playground area with swings, slides, tunnels, and climbing walls. I found a bench just outside the playground area, not far from the parking lot.

The park was relatively empty except for a couple of pre-school children accompanied by either their caregiver or a female parent. In my geographic area, it was becoming more and more common for children to be co-raised by a caregiver or nanny, as both parents continued to pursue their careers. Interestingly, with as much as I've read about stay-at-home dads, I was the only male figure present ... until Ray arrived.

I saw him drive up, his Jeep unmistakable with its "COACH" license plate. He parked the car next to mine and took a minute to exit. He was wearing a sweat suit and a blue New York Yankees baseball cap. I lifted my hand in a partial wave, partial "Here I am" motion.

He walked up to me and said, "Hi."

"Good morning, Ray."

He sat down next to me on the bench and got right to the point. "Where should we start?" Ray asked.

"How about the same place we started when we met back in January? What do *you* want?" I flashed back with a strong dose of sarcasm.

"Touché," Ray said. "I ...."

"How about," I cut in, "explaining why you didn't call me before you left? Why did you just leave a letter?" Now the floodgates were open. "Why didn't you call me when I left a note on your car at the race? Why didn't you let me know that you were going to sell Jo's, *before* you actually sold it? To put it in your own terms, 'What do *you* want?!'"

I stared at Ray, the silence lingering throughout the park, creating a gap that permitted him to choose his response, instead of just reacting.

Ray proceeded passionately, but calmly, "It's not about what I want; it's about what I didn't want, and I learned that from you. As I said to you in the letter, no relationship is one-sided, relationships are created to serve all who are involved. I know you might wonder what you taught me in our short three months, but I did, in fact, learn from you, more than I ever shared.

"What I didn't want, any longer, was the feeling of guilt. I then asked myself, 'What do I want?' and what I realized was that I wanted the feeling of peace."

I just sat there and stared at him in silent wonder. Guilt? Peace? What was he talking about? He seemed to be the most centered person I had ever known. "Do you want to expand upon that?" I asked.

"Yes, now I will," Ray replied, gently tugging on the ring on his left pinkie.

"When we first met, I was closing in on twenty years of living my life without Josephine—twenty years of guilt because I got to live and she didn't. I would have gladly taken the cancer for myself. It was twenty years of trying to figure out what I was going to do without her, twenty years of decomposition, a very slow agonizing deterioration. On top of that, when we met, I also started feeling guilty because I was not practicing what I was preaching. I was out of integrity with myself. I was telling you to be clear on what you wanted and to seek out or create ways to make those things happen, yet I wasn't applying those teachings to myself.

"The first time you entered Jo's, you looked like I felt inside. While it appeared I was extending myself to you, I had actually chosen the table for four in the hopes that someone would join me. Matt, to be perfectly candid with you, I was trying to figure out how to exit this world. After twenty years without my beloved Jo, I didn't want to live another moment longer, until you accepted my invitation to join me at the table. When we met, I was on my computer making adjustments to my will to ensure that everything was in place if I was able to follow through on my thoughts.

"Do you remember when we spoke about being the bird or the statue and how people, when they feel like the statue, in fact are not like the statue in that they always have the ability to choose to move?"

"Sure, it was one of the first things you told me that made me realize I was in command of my life. My ability to choose is ultimately the only way I have control over my life."

"Well, when I said that, I was actually referring to myself and moving myself out of the muck that I had allowed myself to be in for the past twenty years. Until that point, I was making decisions that ultimately let me avoid the pain I associated with saying goodbye. When I spoke with you, I realized it was time to make a different decision."

"Really! I thought you were just some sage spurting out bite-sized pieces of ancient wisdom all directed at a disillusioned piano teacher!"

Ray gave a small smile and responded, "You apparently gave me waaaay too much credit."

"Okay, while I'm surprised to learn of the 'behind the scenes,' you still haven't answered some of my questions."

"Fine, ask away. I will answer as best I can."

"Why didn't you call me before you left?"

"Matt, if I had called you, I would've felt obligated to explain why I was leaving. First, I wasn't really sure what I was doing except that, in an effort to bring some closure into my life, I had to complete Jo's last request of having her ashes deposited in Hawaii. Second, I truly wasn't sure of how long I was going to be gone. Third, if you haven't already surmised, I'm not very good with closure."

"Okay, then why didn't you respond to the letter I left on your car after the Cow Harbor Run?"

"Very simply, I wasn't ready to have what I knew would to be the inevitable conversation we're presently having. But you're very persistent. When you came by my home, I felt cornered, that's why my responses to you were terse. Again, I wasn't ready to see you and one of the things I learned about myself on my sojourn, was that I had to respect my GUT feeling, even if I couldn't explain it to myself or others."

"Sojourn? What's a sojourn?" I asked.

"The standard definition is *to stay somewhere temporarily*. But, as you know, I have my own definitions. For me it meant a solo journey," Ray responded.

"Hmmm, I like the sound of that," I replied.

"Okay, two more questions. Did Camille know you were going on your sojourn?"

"Yes. What she knew was that my first order of business was to create closure with the death of my wife by depositing Jo's ashes in Hawaii. She also knew that I had sold Jo's Café. All the paper work for that occurred in March, just before I left. The decision to sell Jo's was, again, to create closure. When I originally built Jo's, it was to honor my wife, but it started to become an anchor, which kept me from leaving my self-made harbor of despair.

"Camille is a very trusted friend. She was with Jo and me through Jo's fight and ultimate loss to cancer. I made Camille promise that when you came by, all she would do was hand you the letter. It was against *her* better judgment but, based upon your reaction, she respected my request, as I fully expected she would.

"What is your final question?"

"Actually you answered it. It was about the sale of Jo's, but let me ask you one more question."

"Sure."

"Earlier, you said 'to be perfectly *candid* with you.' You didn't say 'to be perfectly *honest* with you.' Knowing how carefully you choose your words, I have to assume this is another *Diamond Distinction*. Will you explain it?"

Ray laughed. "You are extremely observant, that's one of the reasons I always enjoyed, and hope to continue to enjoy, our time together. I always had to be careful about what I said around you. You made me sharpen my sword of communication!

"I'm always honest, but sometimes not so transparent. To say 'to be perfectly *honest* with you' would be predicated upon the fact that somewhere in our relationship I wasn't perfectly honest with you or wouldn't be in the future and that would be a lie. I refuse to lie."

"You said 'I refuse to lie.' Why not just say 'I don't lie.'"

"Because we always have a choice; the word *refuse* acknowledges that choice. My choice is to not lie. Choosing the word *refuse* always reminds me of my preference.

"Okay, Matt, now it's my turn. I have a question for you."

"I'll answer it to the best of my ability," I replied with a bit of a smirk.

"When we first met, I had mentioned that someday I might want to take piano lessons. I declare today is someday. Will you teach me how to play?"

"No, but, if you'd like, I will facilitate you through your own learning of it," I replied.

An important distinction had occurred for me in the time that Ray was gone. I discovered that I really wasn't interested in learning how to teach the piano. Instead, what yielded a much better result was understanding how each of my students best learned at the piano.

And, once again, the lessons began, and this time I was certain they were for the both of us.

CHAPTER 7

I left the park and drove to my home, just fifteen minutes away. NOTES: I felt recharged, empowered, and, very simply, at peace. My relationship with Ray had grown. Our breakdown had ended with a breakthrough. I felt more of an equal, having acted in integrity with my feelings and also knowing that I had made a positive impact in *his* life. I also felt that I was less "held captive" by the limiting beliefs I had continued to hold about authority figures. The proverbial straight jacket had loosened.

While at a stoplight, I caught a glimpse of my face in the rear view mirror; I was smiling. Hmm, smiling. It felt strange to catch myself smiling without having realized I was doing so. Everything in my GUT was telling me I had done the right thing.

I was glad that Diane had challenged me to speak with Ray instead of simply keeping the peace by being non-confrontational and respectful. The time between my conversation with Diane and my conversation with Ray allowed me to *respond* in a way that was fruitful for both Ray and me. Historically, I might have just reacted more emotionally, which usually left me with a result that was less than desirable. That was an important distinction for me, the difference between reacting and responding.

When I respond, there's a gap between the event and my response. That gap can be a moment or a day but, in the gap, in the silence, lies the power to choose what I will say or what I will do. In the gap lies my ability to choose my life instead of simply repeating old patterns by reacting to it. The *gap* was such a powerful idea to me, that I created an acronym for it: **G**rab **A**nother **P**ossibility.

When I react, I function in a more knee-jerk manner. The course of my life becomes a repetition of reactions I've had before and continue to repeat. Responding, especially in emotionally charged situations, has always proven to be better for the outcome.

Upon arriving home, I went into my office, and I found four new phone calls from potential students. I picked up the phone and dialed the first number. A woman answered the phone. "Hello, this is Matt from Higher Ground Music. I'm returning a call from Debra Cavanaugh about piano lessons for her daughter."

I had named my company after a Stevie Wonder song because the song title spoke to my mission of using the study of an instrument to learn about myself and how to achieve all of my goals. The first line of the song was, "People, keep on learning."

"Hello, this is Debra."

"Hi Debra. How are you?"

"Fine thanks. Thank you for getting back to me so quickly."

"Not a problem. Is this a good time to speak with you?"

Over the past few months, after Ray's challenge to me to become more aware of my use of language, I had started paying closer attention to how my words felt as well as to how they may be perceived. I started to find myself feeling bothered when I asked if it was "a good time to speak *to* you." That phrase never felt quite right. It felt like I was lecturing, and I didn't want to do that. I wanted to have a dialogue *with* the person on the other end of the phone. That's when I decided to ask if it was "a good time to speak *with* them." They were two very small words "to" and "with." One separated the communicators; the other united them. It was another *Diamond Distinction*.

"Yes, this is great. I'm free for the next half hour, then I have to pick up my youngest daughter at preschool."

"Is that the daughter you called about for piano lessons?" I asked.

"No, my youngest is four. Do you work with four-year-olds?" Debra asked surprised.

"As a matter of fact, I do."

"Hmm, I had originally called you because I wanted to see if you would evaluate my six-year-old to see if she had any talent for the piano."

"What is her name?" I asked.

"Isabella, but we call her Bella,'" she replied.

Debra's query about talent had struck a nerve with me and, while I knew what she was talking about, it really wasn't an accurate use of language. I was hoping to make a distinction for her, and I was also hoping she was ready to receive it.

"If I may offer my opinion on *talent*, I may be able to make an important distinction for you that will answer your question. Is that okay?"

"Certainly," Debra responded.

"Talent is mined or harvested potential. The way a person takes potential and turns it into talent is through work. In the case of someone studying an instrument, that work is called *practice*. My belief is that *everyone* has the potential to make music and learn the piano. If you're asking how good Bella could be, that will depend on how much she practices.

"Think about a farmer. The seed is the *potential*, the harvested crop is the *talent*. How does the farmer get the seed from potential to harvest?"

Debra replied, "Well, he plants it, waters it, and fertilizes it."

"Exactly, all acts of work," I responded.

There was a silence over the phone that used to scare me, but I had learned to not fill it, as it was usually the person on the other end considering my words.

"Wow, that's really interesting and it makes so much sense. It has such a positive feeling to it! If that is reflective of your philosophy, I already know that I would be interested in having Bella study with you. Plus, you came highly recommend from the Keaton family."

I had been working with all four children in the Keaton family for the past five years. They were an incredibly smart and hard-working family. Because they worked with focus and commitment, they were very successful in all they did: school, sports, family, and music.

"I'll have to thank them when I see them later today."

"Well, we live just around the corner from them. Is there any way you can get us on your schedule today?"

"I'm sorry, but I have two students right after them. Let me speak with them today and see if they can move a little later and, if so, I'll be able to start Bella next week. I don't think it will be a problem because they're older students. Would that be okay?"

"Yes, that would be great!

"What would you do with a four-year-old?" Debra asked.

"What is your four-year-olds name?"

"Sophia."

"The reason many parents and even some teachers do not believe in starting a four-year-old is usually because they feel that the child's attention span cannot last for thirty minutes. And, in the instance of requiring that child to just sit at a piano, they're probably correct.

"What I believe, however, is that learning music is exactly like learning a language. It's a three-fold process. The first step is to learn the *sound* of the language. Think about how Sophia, or for that matter, how anyone learns their native language. What is the first thing they do?"

"Listen?" Debra responded.

"Exactly! They absorb the phrasing and the sounds of the language. Every human being, upon birth, is completely capable of speaking every language. The only determinant of which language becomes that person's native tongue is exposure. If you place an American child in Japan for the first six years of his or her life, they will become fluent in Japanese.

"The same thing happens with the language of music. Children have to be exposed to the language. The language has to get *in their ear*. That's what people mean when they say that a person has a good ear for music. They're saying that the person was exposed to the language of music, and they internally get how it's supposed to sound. So, one of my jobs would be to simply get the language of music in Sophia's ear.

"The next step would be to allow her to explore the instrument through which she will recreate this language. Her first instrument is her voice, so we will sing, and we will also play the piano. I won't bog her down with too much technique as most children find that tedious and boring. My initial goal would be to get her to love playing the piano and making music, by building upon her natural curiosity.

"The final process is linking up the language she has in her ear with the visual representation of that language—reading music. Her reading will be very basic for the first couple of years. Does that make sense to you?"

"Absolutely! Okay, let's give both of my girls a try. Will you be able to fit them both in your schedule?" Debra asked.

"I believe so, but let me give you a call back tomorrow to confirm for next week."

We talked a bit more about my tuition rate, how cancellations were handled, and other boilerplate stuff.

After a healthy dunch (dinner/lunch) of grilled chicken, mixed greens, and brown rice, I headed off to my 2:30 lesson. Today, I was fully inspired to be a guiding light for my students.

When I arrived at the house of my first lesson, the universe must have picked up on my positive energy and sent it to my student before I arrived. Jonathan was waiting at the front door for me with a grin from ear to ear. "Hi, Mr. Matt! I learned the entire melody to a new song on the radio!"

"Wow, Jonathan, I'm proud of you! That's awesome! And do you know what is really cool?"

"I learned the song?" Jonathan replied innocently.

"Yes, but more importantly, look how proud you are of yourself! Doesn't that feel awesome?"

"Yes, I'm really excited!"

"That's your reward for working hard and achieving your goals—those great feelings of excitement and pride!"

As I never believed in giving students trinkets to motivate them to practice, I had to come up with a new way of teaching my students to motivate themselves. After considering what Ray had shared with me nearly a year ago, I decided that the best platform for self-motivation was to teach them about their feelings.

As I told Ray back in February, I knew, by making myself a stern inflexible teacher, I could motivate a student through fear. I began my career with exactly that motivational philosophy. The student would feel frightened and intimidated of me if they hadn't practiced and, therefore, they would practice or quit.

In addition to the realization that I was losing income, I also recognized that I didn't like students being afraid of me and, *most importantly*, I didn't like who *I* was when I motivated through fear. So, I made a conscious decision to rethink my strategy of motivation.

I decided that while it took a longer time to facilitate a student on how to motivate himself with a toward pleasure and pride philosophy, it was gentler and allowed me to act more as a facilitator than a teacher. It also aligned me with my own beliefs, so I was acting in integrity with myself.

When a student didn't achieve a goal, they usually didn't feel proud. Instead of preaching to them that they needed to practice, I simply acted as a coach and a mirror. "Are you happy with how you feel about your preparation for today's lessons? Do you feel proud?"

Most students would answer honestly with a "No."

"Do you want to change that feeling?"

"Yes."

"Then what do you think you could do?"

I had stopped using the word *should* because the word *should* had so many condescending implications. Adults would use the word *should* when they wanted to manipulate a student or child into feeling guilty. I wasn't interested in manipulating my students into feeling anything. I wanted them to become aware of their feelings, decide which feelings they liked and wanted to recreate and which feelings they did not like and wanted to avoid. I then shared with them strategies for consistently creating the feelings they wanted.

Feelings were the feedback, the GPS, the GUT (**G**uidance **U** **T**rust) as Ray had said. That feedback assisted in letting you know if you were on or off course. When something feels good and you feel proud, you're on course. But, when the feedback feels less than desirable, it's a sign that you might want to consider changing directions. My belief was that if I could teach a student how to honor these feelings through my work with them at the piano, then I would be providing them with a compass through which they could successfully and safely navigate anything that came their way in life. I was interested in empowering them.

Usually the student would answer my "What do you think you could do?" question with the word *practice*. They knew that was the correct answer. (Most children are very adept at giving adults and authority figures the answer they want.) I, however, wasn't interested in getting the answer they thought I wanted. I was interested in getting real answers, answers that were true for the student. So, I would go a little further with my questioning.

"Do you need any assistance in creating feelings of pride and success for yourself this week? Do you understand the assignment or are you feeling confused by it? If you're confused, it's my job to give you the information to assist you in not feeling confused."

"No, I know what I have to do; I just need to do it."

"Do you need assistance in making the time to practice?"

"Do you mean have my parents remind me?"

"That could work, if you think it would work for *you*."

"No, I don't want to do that. What if I make a chart and fill in the chart each day I practice? Maybe I could try to do like ninety minutes this week."

"That sounds like an awesome idea to assist you in creating those great feelings of accomplishment! I'm glad you came up with it."

And then the student would go about creating his chart and completing it for the week.

This *student-directed* learning process did not take root quickly. Like the path of an airplane, there were constant corrections throughout the flight. I had once read that an airplane is actually off course for ninety-five percent of its flight! It has to make constant small corrections to accurately arrive at its destination.

Teaching a student to navigate the flight of his own personal growth was exactly the same way. Each week provided feedback on how on or off course the student was. If the student felt proud, he was on course, if he felt anything that was very uncomfortable or not proud, he was off course. My job was to reflect back to him his feelings and then assist him in plotting the upcoming week's course. I was simply a mirror.

Jonathan was a great student because he held himself responsible for the outcome of his efforts. On the occasional times he fell short of his goals, he could forget to treat himself with kindness (as is the way with most people who hold themselves accountable for the results in their lives). In those times, I defined my job title as "protector of his inner being" and tried to ensure that he didn't beat himself up. I simply wanted him to recognize that he didn't like what he was feeling and then to act differently to achieve a different feeling, without the feeling of guilt.

Over my years of teaching, I noticed that adults, when they achieved less then optimal results, were really good at beating themselves up. (I guess practice makes perfect!) Once, when working with an adult student who was on a tirade about her pianistic inequities, I saw a picture on a mantle of a young girl standing next to two adults; I assumed they were the young girl's parents. I asked my student who the people in the picture were. She said, "That's my communion picture with my parents. I asked her, "Would you be so hard on that child?" She abruptly stopped her self-demeaning rant and started to tear up. Hmmm, maybe it's that simple, just have all adults carry a picture of themselves as a child as a reminder to treat that innocent being with gentleness and respect.

As I walked in the house and was saying "Hello" to Jonathan's mom, Jonathan had already run to the piano and started playing his tune. I immediately followed him and watched him sitting proudly at the piano, his nine-year-old legs lightly touching the pedals as his "two-month-old" piano fingers found their way around the keys to recreate the song he had learned by ear.

When he was finished, he looked over to me with a big toothy grin. That was *my* reward. The reward of a student who *knew* he had done a great job. "Jonathan, I LOVED the way you played that melody without stopping. The smooth steady beat made me feel like dancing!"

Even though I wanted my students to be completely self-motivated and internally driven, I was keenly aware that everyone, children and adults alike, still likes to be validated for their achievements.

Jonathan's grinned widened even more.

My day continued as it had started, as if all the stars had aligned simply because I stretched my comfort zone in the morning. The icing on the cake was when I arrived home and Diane had surprised me by coming by my home and making a romantic candlelit dinner. Life was good.

CHAPTER 8

The meal Diane had made was wonderful—shrimp risotto with a nice New Zealand Sauvignon Blanc, a side of wild arugula salad with a simple fresh lemon dressing, and a chocolate soufflé for dessert.

"You look very happy," she said as she served the salad.

"I am. I feel empowered and charged! I had an awesome day."

"So, can I assume you spoke with Ray?" she asked.

"You would be correct in assuming that. We met at Blydenburgh Park this morning at 10:00."

"So, I can also assume that your relationship is intact?" she inquired.

"Yes, but more than just intact. It's better. It feels … more mature. I feel equal to him, not like a star-struck student. It was definitely relationship building, not relationship breaking."

As I thought about my interactions with both my students and other people in my life, I realized that in all interactions, either one of two things were occurring. Walls were either being built or walls were being taken down. When a brick is added to a wall, because communication is either non-existent or non-effective, it creates a barrier. When a brick is taken away from a wall, as all *effective* communication does, it creates an opening, a stronger bond. Once I realized this, my goal was to build relationships by taking down walls and building bonds. My interaction with Ray, in its simplest form, had done this.

This wasn't always easy to do, because in many ways it meant stepping out of my comfort zone. But, when something was running around my head for more than forty-eight hours, I had to act on it. I realized my brain space was limited and any idea that was renting a piece of it needed to be addressed.

"So, in your mind, Ray reacted favorably?" Diane asked.

"Actually, yes, he responded in a way that showed he cared about the relationship. He willingly explained his position and choices. Apparently, I had given him too much credit for being the perfectly wise, omnipotent sage and not enough for being a human being.

"I brought up all the issues that were charged for me—why he hadn't told me he was leaving, why he had sold Jo's, and why he hadn't replied to the note I left on his car after the Cow Harbor Run. He addressed and clarified each. I guess the big motivator for his actions was that he didn't have closure with the death of his wife.

"You know how he said in his letter that relationships aren't just one-sided, they're there to serve all involved?"

"Yes, I remember that. Did he tell you how your relationship served him?" Diane asked.

"Yes. He said that it made him realize he was not practicing what he preached and that he was out of integrity with himself. He realized that that feeling was not the one he wanted and had spent the last several months readjusting his life so he could feel at peace and happy.

"And the kicker was that Ray asked if I would teach him how to play the piano!"

"Sounds like you were more impactful than you expected," Diane replied.

"Yes, I guess you never really know how you affect people."

"I'm really proud of how you took this on. I know it was uncomfortable for you," Diane said.

Even though I was an adult, the acknowledgment of my accomplishment felt good.

"Yeah. Thanks for pushing me to act in spite of the fear."

Sometimes motivation does not take on the uniform of an encouraging cheerleader but instead comes disguised as anger, frustration, or embarrassment. Some people are only motivated when their "teapot" starts to boil over. Anger, frustration, and embarrassment actually can be used for a positive result if you're willing to act responsibly on the feeling, using it to show you what you *don't* want and creating the leverage to go after what you *do* want.

"I would call that true courage," Diane replied.

"How do you mean?" I asked.

"Well, people think that courage is the absence of fear. But if you consider it, there's nothing courageous happening if you're not 'taking on' something bigger than you. I guess, to put it in the terms of Ray's comfort zone diagram, true courage is acting outside of your comfort zone. Courage is the act of responding in the face of fear, not in the absence of it."

Hmm. I had never really considered myself courageous, but in this new light, I guess I could wear that badge.

Our conversation continued through the risotto, after which we both got up and cleared the table. I lit a fire in the fireplace, and we had dessert. I watched Diane's eyes as shadows of the flames danced across her face. She was absolutely beautiful and appeared to be in thought.

I considered writing a love song for her, but I had decided years ago that a career as a successful love-song composer was not in my cards. All the love songs on the radio were victim songs. "If you leave me now, you'll take away the biggest part of me," "I can't smile without you," "Don't let me be lonely tonight," "I know that I can't live without her," "There's no me without you," and the list goes on. The lyrics to my love songs were more along the path of, "I was doing pretty good without you, and now I enjoy sharing our lives together, but if you should choose to leave me, I'll miss you for a while, but I won't die." I was pretty sure that no one was going to buy my songs (at least not the record companies).

"A penny for your thoughts," I asked.

"I was just reflecting on the different feelings I've had for Ray. When you and I first met back in April, you billed him as a sort of savior in your life. And, as I learned more about you and about him, I could understand why. But then, as he ignored your attempts to connect with him, I started to feel annoyed. He began to appear irresponsible to me and that conflicted with my initial view of him.

"Finally, after the race, when you saw him and knew he was in town and then left him the note on his car and he *still* didn't reply, I was feeling angry.

"The final straw was when we were having dinner and you appeared to be defending him. That's when I started feeling resentment toward *him* and frustration with *you!*"

"So, what are your feelings about him now?" I asked.

Diane contemplated my question in silence, exhaled slowly, and replied.

"I'd like to meet him."

CHAPTER 9

Ray and I had set the time for his first piano lesson for 11:00 AM on the upcoming Friday. We were going to meet in my home studio.

NOTES:

Friday morning came and Ray arrived at 10:55.

"Welcome to your first piano lesson!"

"Thanks, Matt. To be candid, I'm feeling both anxious and excited."

"Those sound like appropriate feelings."

Ray smiled a closed-lipped smile and humbly nodded his head.

"Can I interest you in a cup of espresso, cappuccino, or a latté?" I asked.

"I'll take a latté. I still have an hour," Ray replied.

"What do you mean you 'still have an hour'?" I asked.

"When I was in Italy, drinking cappuccino and latte was acceptable up until noon and then they only drank espresso."

"I didn't know that. That's good to put in my mental log for when I visit Italy. I wouldn't want to seem like a foreigner!"

I was glad Ray had scheduled his lesson for today, as a fresh order of Dolce Tazza beans had arrived yesterday. I dispersed exactly 19.5 grams of ground espresso beans from my Vario coffee grinder into a porta filter and loaded the porta filter into my Quick Mill Vetrano espresso machine. While the perfect twenty-seven-second two-ounce espresso shot was dripping, creating the perfect crema, I got to work on stretching the milk.

Many people believe a good latté is one with a lot of froth or foam in the cup, but that's not correct. The purpose of steaming the milk is to add tiny micro bubbles of air, thereby stretching the milk into a silky cream-like texture. If it is done correctly, it will enable the barista the chance to make a design, called "latté art." I had only mastered the most basic design, the leaf.

Before pouring the milk, I brought the cup to Ray (once the milk was poured, the cup was usually filled to the top and could spill.) The milk poured beautifully and, as the cup started to fill, I gently moved the milk pitcher back and forth creating long thin leaf petals and, with a final run down the middle of the cup, cut the leaves in half resulting in a perfect leaf design.

"Wow! I haven't seen a barista do that since I was in California! Quite impressive, Matt. If I had known you were that good I would've hired you to work at Jo's!" Ray exclaimed.

"Well, thanks, Ray. I've wasted a lot of espresso and milk mastering the humble leaf. It's taken me quite a while, so I appreciate the validation! Had you offered me the position when we first met, when I was in that tenuous time between choosing a new career or continuing to work as a piano teacher, I might have actually taken you up on the offer."

I went back to the machine, made myself a latté, and joined Ray at my kitchen table.

We drank our lattés in silence, the silence shared by two people who were comfortable enough with each other that words were not necessary in order to communicate.

After several minutes, I asked Ray if he would like to get started on his path of music making.

"Yes, let's do it."

We put our cups in the sink. As we moved to my studio, the doorbell rang. I wasn't expecting anyone, so I was surprised to have a visitor.

I answered the door to find Diane.

"Morning!" she said with a smile that reminded me today was a wonderful day to be alive.

"Good morning, Di. I wasn't expecting you."

"Do you have a visitor?" Diane said with a look over my shoulder.

"As a matter of fact, I do. Ray is starting his piano lessons today. He's inside."

"Really! I didn't realize he was starting so soon."

"Well, you know me. When someone says they want to do something, I commit them to a day and a time!"

About ten years ago, I had taken a personal development course that made an interesting distinction. You could create your life from either the circumstances that surrounded and interacted with you or you could create your life from your commitment to achieve what you desired. Working from the circumstance of "when I have the time" or "when I'm richer/retired/weigh less/have more knowledge (or whatever!) usually created no results because no one ever really has the optimal conditions of time/money/health. Working from circumstances usually means working from excuses and *not* having what you wanted.

The only way to truly accomplish your goals is to create the commitment by creating a time for them to happen. That's why when people tell me they want to do something I always make a date with them. In the case of learning a new skill, such as playing the piano, the date created a commitment to *start* the learning process.

When my friends would say, "Hey, let's go out to dinner sometime," I would take out my calendar and reply, "Sure, when?" They usually looked at me in bewilderment. Apparently, they weren't really interested in having dinner together but were letting me know, on some level, they wanted to continue our relationship (usually sans dinner). "Sometime" is never unless a date is put on the calendar.

"Would I be imposing if I came in to say 'Hi'?" Diane asked.

In a way, I felt she would be, but if this was the meeting fate had arranged, who was I to get in its way?

"No, I wanted you two to finally meet so now is as good a time as ever." (It was certainly better than "sometime.")

Diane walked in behind me as I escorted her to my studio.

As we entered the room, Ray turned from the piano. The moment Diane and Ray's eyes met, they were filled with recognition. Diane's mouth and eyes widened, eyebrows raised; the corners of Ray's mouth rose into a smile.

Their recognition had little to do with the stories I shared with them about the other. Their recognition was as if they had already met and, in fact, they already had.

Before I was able to properly introduce the two most important people from the past year of my life, Diane spoke and broke the silence.

"You're Ray? Ray Mandino?"

"Yes, I'm Ray. It's a pleasure to meet you … again."

"Yes, yes it is," Diane replied.

"You're Matt's Diane?" Ray asked.

"Yes, I'm Matt's Diane."

"It appears you two have already met," I interjected with confusion. "Would either of you feel comfortable bringing me up to speed?"

Again, Diane was the first to speak. "Matt, do you remember when you ran the Cow Harbor Run and I was speaking with a gentleman as you came through the finish line?"

"Yes. I think you said he was one of the top three finishers in the 70-79 categ ... wait, was that Ray?" I pointed, "this Ray?!"

"Yes, this is him!" Diane exclaimed.

Ray just sat at the piano bench as all of this seeped in. He was simply smiling.

"And why are you smiling?" I asked him.

"Well, first because I find it incredible that the woman I was speaking with at the race was *your* Diane, this Diane! Of all the possible people to start a conversation with that day, we chose each other. It's a small world and it's working perfectly.

"But, what I never told you, because I hadn't known that the woman at the race and Diane were one and the same, was that Diane's kind spirit and even some of her physical features, reminded me of Josephine. When I met Diane at the race, it was an affirmation that I was on the right path."

When Ray said this, I expected him to grab the ring on his pinkie finger as he always did when he thought or talked about his deceased wife. This time, he didn't.

"How did you know you were *on the right path* when you met Diane at the race?" I asked him.

"The same way you *know* anything, Matt—because it felt right. More accurately, in this case, the *right* feeling was the feeling of peace. In the past when I've had reminders of Jo and her absence in my life, I would feel empty, sad, or depressed. This time I had a twinge of that emptiness, as I will always expect to have, but my prevailing feeling was peace and that's a feeling I wanted.

"Before my sojourn, I always felt that if I didn't feel guilty or depressed when I remembered Jo, I was giving up on her, that somehow she would vaporize into nothingness. In reality, what I actually had to do was *surrender*. Many people liken the word surrender to quitting, but the two ideas are completely different. For me, at this point in my life, it's the most important *Diamond Distinction* of all.

"Quitting has frustration and resistance attached to it. It lacks acceptance; there is an emotional immaturity to it. Surrendering, in contrast, lacks *resistance*. Surrendering is filled will love of yourself, acceptance, and forgiveness. I finally accepted that Jo's life was not my life and while we were as close as a husband and wife could be, we were different people with different life paths who had chosen to share our lives together. We were not in each other's lives to fill a missing piece; we were complete beings on our own. We were not the same person and no amount of self-inflicted torture would bring her back. I finally surrendered and, as a result, I gave myself *my own* life back."

Ray reached into the back pocket of his pants and pulled out his wallet. Reaching behind his license, he pulled out a clear folder of pictures. Unlike the rest of the planet, his pictures did not reside on his mobile phone, as he didn't have one. He still had hard copies of them in those clear plastic protectors.

He took out the plastic protector and there in the front was a picture of a beautiful woman. Petite with dark chestnut hair, beautiful brown eyes that sparkled with life and a smile that clearly lit up the world around her; all that I had imagined her to be based upon Ray's descriptions of her.

"This is my Jo," Ray said with a smile.

"Diane, so much about your spirit reminds me of Jo," Ray said.

I listened to his tone with the ears of a trained musician and did not detect the slightest hint of sadness. I sensed peace.

Together, Diane and I moved closer to look at the picture more carefully.

"She was beautiful," Diane said.

"Yes, she was, both on the outside AND on the inside. Her outer beauty was just a reflection of her inner kindness," Ray agreed.

"Well, I just wanted to stop by and drop off these cookies I made for Matt. I guess he'll have to share them with you now, Ray. It was a pleasure meeting you," Diane said.

"I'm very happy to have officially been introduced to you, and thank you for the cookies!"

I walked Diane to the door and, as I was giving her a kiss goodbye, I heard the piano. Ray was tinkling out his rendition of "The Nearness of You."

After Diane left, I waited outside of my studio because Ray was still playing. I often did this when I was at a student's home by pretending I had to use the bathroom. I would excuse myself and tell the student to continue playing. But, instead of using the bathroom, I would just wait around the corner in another room. Most of the time the student would perform incredibly better simply because he relaxed from "having to play it perfectly for his teacher." His inner critic would be quiet and the student would be able to demonstrate his true ability without pressure. I waited for Ray to finish.

When Ray had completed his performance, I reentered the room and validated his flow and internal sense of beat. "I liked the way you were true to the beat more than the correct notes."

"What do you mean?" he asked.

"Well, many people, when they're learning an instrument, try to play all the correct notes regardless of how those notes flow. Music is the organization of sound over *time*. Most people give preference to the correct notes instead of the correct time, which yields a mechanical choppy sound. It is so much nicer to listen to someone play who gives preference to the *time* over the notes. Sure, there are some wrong notes, but the *flow* of the notes is present and that's what makes it music. I liked how you did that."

"That's funny, because what I heard was all the notes I was missing," Ray replied.

"Let me put that in perspective for you. You played pro baseball, correct?" I asked rhetorically.

"Yes," Ray answered anyway.

"And would you say that a batter who had a batting average of .850 was a good batter?"

"Well, no I wouldn't because that's not possible," he replied.

"I understand that, but hypothetically, would you say he was good?"

"Yes. Any batter batting with an average of .350 is considered exceptional, so your hypothetical batter would be beyond a superstar," Ray said.

"Well, do you think that you played about eighty-five percent of the notes in the song correctly?" I asked.

"Yes ... got it! Now I know where you're going. So I would be a .850 batter in major league baseball and would be considered a super superstar, yet on the piano, I judge myself by the fifteen percent of the notes I missed. Nicely done. I like your analogy," Ray replied.

"Yes, superstar pro ball players actually *strike out* sixty-five percent of the times at bat. That's like a piano player missing sixty-five percent of the notes! Now I'm certainly not condoning playing sixty-five percent of the notes incorrectly, but to penalize your enjoyment of playing by only recognizing all the wrong notes you played is not fair to yourself or effective for motivating you to progress."

I basked a moment in my own spotlight, serendipitously enjoying the equal ground that Ray and I were on.

We continued our lesson covering a bunch of different ideas and, after about an hour, Ray decided he had enough to play with until our next lesson, which I encouraged him to schedule for the next week.

"Why don't I just give you a call to schedule a lesson when I feel I've got a grip on the concepts we explored today?"

"That simply doesn't work because you don't have any pressure to get something done. Making a commitment and then working out the circumstances to follow through on your commitment will always allow you to achieve more."

"I understand. Next Friday at 10:00 AM then?"

"That works. Have a great week. Call me if you have any questions so that you can get the most out of the seven days until your next lesson. I'll let you leave with the same final statement I say to all my students. In seven days, you'll be seven days older. Will you also be seven days better, seven days closer to playing the piano the way you want?"

Ray nodded his head and smiled.

CHAPTER 10

Ray arrived the following Friday at exactly 10:00 AM. We had NOTES: our coffee, quickly re-establishing the rapport of our relationship. I asked him about his successes at the piano throughout the week.

"Well, one of the things I was successful at learning, was that I'm very good at being impatient with myself. My brain knew what it wanted my hands and my fingers to do, but my limbs did not respond with anywhere near the speed that my brain was requesting!"

I replied, "Yep, practicing can definitely pit you up against yourself! When you're learning something physical, and the piano is a physical instrument, no matter how much you understand something, you still have to train your muscles to demonstrate the knowledge. I think Sam Snead, a famous golfer, said it best. He said, 'Practice gives your muscles brains.'"

"I actually saw Sam Snead play when I was younger, but I have never heard that quote. It seems very apropos."

"It's like riding a bike, Ray. You can be the world's greatest physicist and completely understand the mechanics behind forward momentum and balancing a bicycle, but the *only* way to actually learn how to ride it, is to get on a bike, inclusive of the bumps and bruises you're almost guaranteed to experience in your learning process!"

"Yep, that's a good description of how I felt this week. Lots of bumps and bruises. I just didn't expect them to come from learning the piano!"

"Ray, let me ask you something. Why did you ask me to teach you the piano?"

"Do you mean why did I ask *you* or why did I choose to learn the piano?"

"Why did you choose to learn the piano?"

"When I was on my sojourn, as I had told you, I realized that my life had not ended, although I was living it as though it had. I was in a diner in Hawaii, just after I had scattered Jo's ashes. I was sitting at a table next to a woman who was probably ten years my senior. She had a stack of college textbooks and appeared to be writing out flashcards. I asked her if she was a teacher. Her response caught me off guard. She smiled and said, 'No, I'm an undergraduate student.'

"'Really!' I said with surprise. 'What are you studying?'

"She replied, 'I'm becoming an attorney.'

"I asked her what year she was in, and she told me she was a sophomore! Imagine that! Starting college and on such a rigorous path in the last quarter of her life.

"So, I had to ask her how she came to this decision. 'What made you decide to start your college education?'

"Her reply hit me right between the eyes. She told me that she was taking stock of her life and simply asked herself, 'What's next?'

"'What's next?' Imagine that—asking that question at seventy-eight years old!

"So, since I believe that nothing occurs by accident, I took her words to heart and asked myself the same question. That's how and when I decided to start my piano lessons. And, since you're probably the only piano teacher I know, you were my logical choice."

"Oh, great; don't I feel honored. Chosen due to a lack of other options."

"Well, that and also because I knew who you were and what you stood for as a person."

"And you still chose me?"

"Yes, in spite of all that, I *still* chose you." Ray said with a smile.

"So, what are you hoping to get as a result of learning the piano?" I asked.

"The joy of simply being a student."

"I understand. With that said, let's stop talking about making music and let's make some music. If you'll allow me one more quote from another famous man, I believe it perfectly sums up my philosophy of learning and how we will proceed with our lessons."

"Fire away, Teach." Ray said.

"'Tell me and I forget. Teach me and I remember. Involve me and I learn.'"

"That's wonderful. Who said it?" Ray asked. "I want to write it down in my iPad."

"Benjamin Franklin."

Ray took out his iPad and jotted down the quote I had just shared.

We then proceeded to the piano. I had Ray adjust the bench to the proper distance, take a relaxed deep breath, and gently place his hands on the keyboard, setting the first blocks in the foundation of his pre-playing ritual. Rituals are important because they set your mind and spirit to the proper state to do whatever it is you are about to do. I learned this from one of my martial arts partners, Kenji. Kenji was a student from Japan.

One Saturday morning Kenji and I had gotten together at his home to workout. I had brought my *gi* pants (the traditional pants worn by karate practitioners) and a t-shirt. Kenji, however, put on his full martial arts uniform—*gi* pants and top and his *obi* (the belt that keeps the gi top closed.) I thought this was odd because, besides holding the gi top together, the belt also stated your rank in the *dojo* (the karate school). We didn't need to have our rank stated because we were just friends working out together. We were both the same rank so, to me, putting on an *obi* was a moot point. I asked him why he was in full uniform.

He replied, "When I put on my full *gi*, *obi* included, it sets me in the right frame of mind to be attentive to what I'm about to do. The ritual of putting on my *gi* tells my mind and body I'm about to train. It prepares me internally."

That made sense. Rituals. Religions have them, as their call to prayer sets the congregation in the right frame of mind. The batting ritual of a baseball player is easily recognizable. "Adjust my left batting glove then my right, next interlock my fingers. Tap the left cleat with the bat then the right. Point my left toe into the dirt, push it around in a circle like I'm putting out a cigarette butt, lift the bat up and out pointing over the pitcher's head, wiggle my hips, position my rear leg in place. Load the bat in place. Now, I'm ready to bat."

I had Ray review his pre-playing ritual several times so that it would become, well, more of a ritual—automatic and spirit invoking.

For the next hour, the piano lesson progressed with little talking and much modeling and mimicking. By the end, Ray's playing was much improved. He was a great student! He knew how to learn. A large part of my mission was teaching a student, not just *what* to learn but *how* to learn, how to become their own teacher, how to set up their internal learning environment for success. The *what* was easy; much of my time was spent on the *how*. I needed to make sure that they owned the information I shared with them. If they merely rented it, they would always need me in order to progress. But if they *owned* it, they could continue to grow even without a teacher.

As the lesson came to an end, I asked Ray to demonstrate what he had learned. He took a deep breath, demonstrated his pre-playing ritual, and started to play "Imagine" by John Lennon. When he was done, the room was silent, except for the visual applause that radiated from the ear-to-ear grin on his face.

"Not to sound condescending, but I'm proud of you," I said to him.

"I'm proud of me," was his simple response. It was as though he had never heard those words before.

CHAPTER 11

One of the things I was starting to recognize in my new NOTES: heightened awareness of my teaching was a heightened awareness of my life in general. As I started to trust my GUT more and more, I was starting to see small coincidences that began to feel like more than just chance happenings. I was starting to feel an interconnectedness about occurrences that, at first, appeared to be unrelated. Sometimes my ability to see the connectedness occurred days or weeks later. (I guess 20-20 hindsight has its merits.) Things started to appear less random. The control over my life was clearly rooted in my responses to life's random occurrences, but I was starting to see these occurrences as more purposeful and felt more empowered to control my life through the choices I made.

My friend Sal had invited Diane and me to his house for dinner with his family on Sunday. Diane and I didn't have plans so, after explaining Sal's heritage to her and the ramifications of this invitation, we gladly accepted. Sal was from an Italian family, and an invitation to his home for dinner on a Sunday meant arriving at two in the afternoon and feasting until seven or eight at night. It was an event!

I met Sal in college; we were roommates. As a first-semester college freshman, the month of December arrived with a good dose of homesickness. One night, after a grueling study session while kicking back with a few beers, we started sharing our family traditions, anticipating our upcoming break. When it was Sal's turn, he spoke about how his family would eat from two

83

in the afternoon until late into the night. It was my first introduction to the Italian way of celebrating the holidays.

Being from a family that was of the "Heinz 57" variety, we had our traditions and specific foods associated with them, but we had nothing that remotely resembled Sal's feast. My family ate our ham with one or perhaps two side dishes and that was our holiday meal. Sal's family seemed to prepare an entire restaurant menu. So I challenged Sal. "Do you mean that if I showed up on your doorstep at 11:00 PM on Christmas night there would be food on the table?!" Sal proudly replied, "Yes, and I think I could even tell you what it would be! My family and I would be sitting around playing cards and reheating the lasagna we had around 5:00 PM."

Since Sal only lived forty-five minutes from my hometown, I took him up on his offer, albeit without telling him I was going to do so. On Christmas day, at 11:00 PM of my freshman year in college, I showed up on his parent's doorstep. His mother answered the door, smiled unfazed and said, "You must be Matt. Come on in, Sal's been expecting you. There's food on the table. I'll get you a plate and some utensils."

Food on the table was an understatement! There was lasagna, fruits, pies, dozens of varieties of cookies, meatballs, and sausages. I had died and gone to Italian heaven and I wasn't even Italian! And there was Sal, with a knowing grin and a welcoming hug, playing cards with his dad, uncles, and cousins. Over these late-night snacks and a poker game, I found out that the usual, non-holiday Sunday party typically ended around 8:00 PM.

From that day on Sal and I had become close friends. Sal pursued a degree in computer programming and got a job with a large firm on the island, and I followed my career as a music teacher, opening my own company after a short stint in the public school system. Sal had continued this tradition of food and family with his own family and would "unplug" each Sunday to cook, eat, and reunite.

On Sunday morning, I ran an extra two miles in preparation for the caloric onslaught I was anticipating throughout the rest of the day. Diane and I arrived promptly at 2:00 PM and were greeted by Sal's wife, Jacqui, and their two children, Francesca and Bianca. Francesca was seven and Bianca was four. Jacqui was behind them as they answered the door. "Hi, Uncle Matt!" exclaimed Francesca as she gave me a big hug.

From what Sal explained to me, Italian families have *many* people who are not related to them who are their "aunts" and "uncles." It was a sign of comfortable respect that was taught and it worked for me. I wasn't comfortable with his children addressing me by my last name, nor was I okay with them just calling me Matt. Uncle Matt worked just fine and it had the added benefit of making me feel like family.

Kneeling to her level, I gave Francesca a big hug, "Hello Francesca! Where's your younger sister? I don't see her."

Bianca was standing right next to Francesca exclaiming, "Here I am. Here I am!"

"I can hear her voice, but where is she?" I teased as I placed my hand above my eyes and looked around the room.

"I'm right next to 'Chesa!" Bianca squealed.

I looked down to meet her eyes, "Oh, there you are. When did you get here?"

"I live here! I'm always here, Uncle Matt!" Bianca exclaimed through her giggle.

I gave Bianca a hug and she wrapped her little arms around my neck in the most welcoming manner any human being deserved.

I stood up, smiled at Jacqui, we hugged, and I thanked her for having us over.

"Who's that?" Francesca finally asked, pointing to Diane.

"This is Diane, my girlfriend," I replied.

"Uncle Matt has a girlfriend. Uncle Matt has a girlfriend!" Bianca sang, as she twirled around the room.

Francesca tugged on Jacqui's pants and Jacqui leaned down for Francesca to whisper in her ear. Jacqui whispered back and Francesca nodded.

Later I found out that Francesca wanted to know if she was supposed to call Diane, "Aunt Diane" and Jacqui, not wanting to make Diane feel uncomfortable, told her that wasn't necessary … yet.

"Hi, Diane." Francesca said as she extended her hand for a shake.

Diane squatted and extended her hand, "Hello, Francesca. I'm really happy to meet you. I love the flowers on your dress."

"Thank you," Francesca replied.

"I have more dresses like this one, but this is my favorite. Do you want to see my other dresses?" Francesca continued.

"Sure, if it's okay with your mom," Diane replied.

"Absolutely." Jacqui responded.

"I have a pretty dress too, but I'm not wearing it," Bianca chimed in.

"I can see you're not wearing a dress, but I do love your sweater, especially with the ice skaters on it. Would you like to show me your dresses, too, Bianca?" Diane asked.

"Yes, yes, yes!" Bianca exclaimed, as she continued her "happy dance" around the room.

Sal beckoned from another room, "Hey, Matt, come on into the kitchen. I'm just finishing up some of the appetizers."

I gave Jacqui my coat and strolled to the kitchen where I was greeted by a hug and a glass of wine.

"Great to see you," Sal said with a welcoming smile.

"I heard Diane, but I believe she has been kidnapped by my daughters. With Francesca's dress collection, we might never see her again!" Sal said.

I hadn't yet introduced Diane to any of my friends, they had only heard about her. I was sure that part of the purpose of Sal's invite was to meet her.

"Hopefully, the girls will return her before we run out of wine," Sal continued.

Sal was quite the amateur chef. He often said that if he hadn't gotten a degree in computer science, he would've gone to culinary school. He was constantly trying different recipes, and I was always happy to be his guinea pig.

"What's on the menu today?" I asked.

"Straight up Italian: Peasant Soup, pasta marinara, meatballs, sausages, and *braciole* (an Italian meat roll of different herbs, spices, and cheese), a simple salad, and then Chicken Francesé with broccoli rabe. Jacqui made vanilla bean crème brûlée for dessert."

"Well, it smells great. I coached Diane to fast for the past two days in anticipation of what you were going to prepare! I'm glad you're not going to disappoint."

Sal laughed. Jacqui joined us as we waited for the kidnapped Diane to be returned. A few moments later, Francesca and Bianca skipped into the kitchen with Diane, one on each side of her, holding her hands. All three were smiling.

"I like Diane!" Bianca exclaimed.

"So do I," I replied. Diane smiled and leaned into me.

"Hello, Diane, I'm Sal. It's a pleasure to finally meet you," Sal said as he extended his hand, to which Diane responded by giving him a hug.

"She's got my seal of approval," Sal said as he released the hug.

Diane smiled. Since the girls had released her hands, this time when she leaned into me, she also wrapped her arm around my waist.

"Mine too. You're wonderful with kids. I love the way you relate to our two girls. You have a very special way with them," Jacqui chimed in.

Relate. Hmmm.

"Thank you. Your girls are very welcoming and easy to have fun with. You guys appear to be incredible parents," Diane said, returning the compliment.

"Appearances can be misleading. Give the girls a chance. They'll show you what they're really made of once they get to know you," Sal said with a smile.

Jacqui jumped in, "Well, thanks for that acknowledgment. To us, it's the most important job we have."

"Would you like a glass of wine?" Sal asked Diane.

"Absolutely," she replied.

"Red or white?"

"Whatever you have open is fine."

"Both are open. The red is a Pennywise Pinot Noir and the white is a New Zealand Sauvignon Blanc."

"Then I'll take a glass of the red, thank you."

We each had our glasses and I proposed a toast, thanking them for the invitation and their hospitality.

As we continued sipping our wines around the kitchen counter, appetizers of cured meats, cheeses, and olives started appearing. The girls ate everything, except the olives, which Bianca had declared as "yucky."

After forty-five minutes of appetizers, Sal invited us into the dining room. The table was set with special dishes and glasses and there were nametags written with crayons in "child font."

"Francesca, did you make the name tags?" I asked.

"Yes, Uncle Matt."

"Bianca, did you help?"

"I put them in the dishes!" Bianca said, with a big grin.

"Nice job, girls. I love the way you help your mom and dad," I replied.

Sal brought out the Peasant Soup. It was a roasted garlic bread soup and was a perfect winter dish.

"Wow, I really like this!" Diane exclaimed after taking her first sip.

"See, I told you he could cook," I said to Diane.

"Thank you. I'm glad you like it. It was my grandmother's recipe," was Sal's humble reply.

Next came out the pasta and gravy meats.

Diane turned to me, "You weren't kidding about a lot of food."

"Oh, we still have three more courses," Sal replied. "Pace yourself."

After the pasta, Francesca and Bianca asked if they could be excused to play in their room.

"Please put your pasta plates in the dishwasher, then you may go and play," Sal replied.

"Do you want to play with us?" Bianca asked Diane.

"I'd like to spend some more time with your mom and dad. Would you let me play with you after we finish eating our chicken?"

"Sure!" Bianca replied.

We helped clear the pasta course and had the salad.

There was a breather after the salad during which Sal started working on the chicken.

"Do you need any help, my friend?" I asked.

"Sure, let's create a culinary masterpiece. You can chop the shallots and slice the garlic—thin slices, please."

"Not a problem."

Create ... create ....

Relate, create. Nice rhyme.

Sal gave me a chef's knife and I cut through the shallots and garlic with precision. I was much more comfortable with tools that did not have to be plugged in.

Relate, create.

After seasoning both sides of the chicken breast, then dipping them in flour and egg, Sal dropped them in the hot olive-oil-coated pan. The syncopated sizzle of the chicken hitting the hot oil rang throughout the kitchen.

"Done with the shallots?"

"Yep, here you go, Chef," I replied.

"Great. Want to slice some lemons for me?"

"Sure thing. How thick do you want the slices?"

"Quarter inch will be fine."

As Sal finished cooking each of the chicken breasts, he transferred them to a plate in the oven keeping them warm on a low heat while he prepared the sauce. He dropped the shallots in the pan from which the chicken just came, gave them a quick stir, added some butter and flour, let it cook until it was blonde, and then deglazed the pan with white wine. After raising the heat, he added some chicken stock, then the sliced lemons, and a spoonful of capers.

Meanwhile, he dropped the broccoli rabe into a pot of boiling water, quickly blanching them. After they had cooked, he moved them to a pan in which he was sautéing the garlic I had sliced. A sprinkle of salt, a grind from the pepper mill, transfer to a warm serving plate, arrange the chicken and its sauce on another serving platter, and the chicken course was ready to be served.

"Do you want me to get Francesca and Bianca?" I asked.

"Sure. You can ask them if they want some Chicken Francesé. They may not, in which case they can continue playing."

I walked up to the girl's bedroom and knocked.

"Enter the princess' castle," Francesca announced, in her best English accent.

"Hello, young princesses! It's Prince Matt. Your dad, the king and court chef, wanted me to tell you that he's putting the Chicken Francesé on the table and would like to know if you wanted some."

"Chicken 'Chesa? I love Chicken 'Chesa!" Bianca exclaimed.

They both ran down the stairs and sat at the table.

I was surprised at how the girls ate everything the adults ate. Many of the students I taught were prepared special meals if they didn't like what the parents were serving, as though they lived in a restaurant.

"Wow, you girls are great eaters! What's your favorite food we ate today?" I asked.

"I like the cream burly dessert Mommy made!" Bianca chimed.

"We haven't eaten that yet," Francesca corrected.

"I know, but it's still my favorite!" Bianca defended.

Jacqui laughed and thanked Bianca for the compliment and then asked her what food she liked best between the soup, pasta, salad, and chicken.

"I liked the pasta and meatballs," Bianca replied.

"I like the chicken and the broccoli rabe," Francesca responded.

"Really? What do you like best about them?" I continued.

"I like the way the broccoli rabe is a little crunchy and the chicken is lemony-salty," Francesca explained.

"I like how first I eat the pasta and then the meatballs feel round in my mouth!" Bianca offered.

"Wow, I love how you both explained what was special about the foods to you," I validated.

Apparently, they were finished with both their meals *and* my questioning, because Francesca asked if they could go back to playing and if Diane would join them.

"Diane isn't finished with her plate yet. I'm sure once she's done, she'll come and play with you," Jacqui replied, coming to Diane's defense.

"Wow, my mom makes you finish your plate too? I thought you were an adult," Francesca questioned.

We all laughed, caught by surprise at her interpretation of Jacqui's words.

"I'm still enjoying the food your dad prepared. Once I finish, I'll come in to join you," Diane said in defense of Jacqui.

"Okay," Bianca said as she slid off her chair and under the table.

When Diane finished her chicken, she and Jacqui went to the girl's bedroom as promised.

I turned to Sal and said, "That's incredible how the girls know so much about food. I'm amazed."

"It's just a matter of educating them. We've never taken them to a fast food restaurant. At this age, they only know what they're taught. You know, sometimes people compliment us on how well the girls speak, even on the vocabulary they use. But to Jacqui and me, it's nothing special."

"What do you mean?" I asked.

"Well, if you speak baby talk to a child, they will think the way to communicate is baby talk. We just educate them the way we want them to be educated. If you educate them about good food, they will want good food. If you educate them about good vocabulary, they will use good vocabulary. It's really not difficult. It's just like a saying we have in the computer programing field—G.I.G.O., which stands for Garbage In, Garbage Out."

Educate them. Educate them.

By now all of the girls had returned and Bianca was doing her happy dance and chanting, "Time for the cream burly. Time for the cream burly."

I turned to Sal and said, "I guess you guys haven't yet told her the proper French pronunciation of crème brûlée!"

He gave me a friendly one-armed shove. "Jerk."

As expected, the night ended around 7:30. Diane and I said our goodbyes. This time, when Diane knelt down to say goodbye, both Bianca and Francesca gave her a hug. It looked like Diane didn't want to let them go.

"If you want to come back and play with us, that would be okay," Francesca offered.

"Yeah, come play with us tomorrow," Bianca mimicked her older sister.

"I'd love to come see you both again. Maybe when the weather gets nicer we can all go to the park together," Diane offered.

"Yeah, let's go tomorrow!" Bianca chimed.

"Well, not tomorrow, but we would like to see Diane again," Jacqui said as she tossed me a sideways glance.

"I don't think that will be a problem," I replied, as I reached for Diane's hand.

"Thank you for everything. We had a great time," I said as I hugged Sal.

As we were driving away, I honked once and waved goodbye.

Diane was quiet. So was I. I was deep in thought and it appeared that so was she.

"What are you thinking about?" I asked.

"I was just thinking how wonderful a family they are. The girls are incredibly polite and smart. I love the way they enjoyed all the food we enjoyed and that they sat and ate with us. That was really special."

"I agree. When you were upstairs with them, I asked Sal about their eating habits and he said it was simply a matter of educating them about ...."

"About what?" Diane asked.

"... about food, but that's not why I stopped," I continued.

"What are you thinking about?" Diane queried.

"It's not what I was thinking about, it was because I wasn't thinking about it that my brain just put some pieces together.

"You know how I've been sharing with you how I'm starting to see more connections in my life, like things that belong together that at first appeared to be unrelated?"

"Yes."

"Well, it just happened. Tonight, besides the good food and company, three words have imprinted themselves on my brain. And just now, my brain linked them," I replied.

"And those words are?"

"When Jacqui complimented you on how you interacted with Francesca and Bianca, she said she liked the way you *related* to them. That's the first word—*relate*. The second word was *create*. When I went inside to help Sal with the chicken, he said 'Let's *create* a culinary masterpiece.' And the final word was *educate*."

"So, what's so special about those three words, besides that they rhyme and contain the verb we just participated in?" Diane asked, alluding to the word "ate."

"It's funny! They're nothing as individual words but, in a sequence, they describe what you and I do that makes us good facilitators. First, we *relate* to our students. We create good rapport, like you squatting down to speak with the girls. People would say you 'got to their level.' But you didn't just do that physically; you did it verbally and emotionally as well. You related on so many different planes to them that they truly got that you cared about them. It reminds me of something Ray said to me, 'People don't care how much you know until they know how much you care.'

"Next, we *create*. We create an environment in which learning can occur. Sometimes it's firm, sometimes it's compassionate, and sometimes it's comical. But what's imperative is that we create an *optimal* learning environment. And *then* and only then do we *educate* them.

"Many teachers have the whole process backwards. They try to educate first, and then try to create an optimal learning environment through fear motivation and, if it's really poor teaching, they never ever get to the relate part! They never learn a single thing about their student outside of how they function within the subject matter they're teaching."

"Hmmm, no more wine for you! Did you really just come up with that?" Diane asked.

"I don't feel like I came up with it. I feel like it just 'arrived' or came to me. That's what I mean, lately I just let my mind gather information and it comes up with stuff on its own. I'm not trying to come up with stuff; I just can't help it."

"If you were an athlete, they would say you're in the zone," Diane offered.

"Yes, I know about the zone for athletes and even for musicians, but I've never experienced it as a general life concept. It's as though the magic of life exposes itself and your path is lit with halogen runway lights. You just have to be aware of the signs, signs that show up as gentle nudges from your GUT. The process feels effortless."

CHAPTER 12

I looked forward to my Monday lessons. Come to think about it, since I changed my perspective and clarified my mission as an educator, I looked forward to all of my lessons. I found that even on days I didn't necessarily want to teach, teaching focused me and gave my day a sense of value. In this way, my students were probably serving me more than I was serving them. No relationship is one-sided.

Monday was especially enjoyable, because three of my eight students had been with me for at least the past seven years. My relationships with them had strong foundations, so we could quickly proceed to music making.

As I started to think more about the relate-create-educate rhyme that had been running through my head since dinner at Sal and Jacqui's home, I started to recognize that the reason it had connected for me was that I was simply labeling something I had always used in my teaching. I was recognizing that which had already been there.

Some educators I knew thought that their primary job was to simply disseminate subject knowledge. Unless the subject was the student with whom I was working, for me that was the *last* step in the process!

Knowledge is something people can find in a book. If a person can read, they can find knowledge at their local library, through the Internet, or at a bookstore. What books cannot do, is customize the learning experience to the needs of the learner.

That's where the art of teaching or facilitating comes in. Facilitating a student through the acquisition of knowledge for themselves is a lot more challenging than simply relaying information found in a book. Eventually, once the student gathers effective strategies for learning, they will not need their teacher to continue to "babysit" them to continue to learn. I'd say sixty percent of my work with new students is about removing learning obstacles or correcting ineffective learning patterns that block this process from happening.

The first stage in my relationship with a student, especially with a new student, is to create rapport. *Relate.*

I'm comfortable meeting and speaking with just about any student or person because I have a toolbox of skills for doing so. Many people think I'm able to create rapport simply because I have a good personality. While this may or may not be true, my ability to create rapport comes more from a learned set of skills than simply from a good set of genes.

Growing up, I didn't have this skill set. As a matter of fact, I was one of the boys at the school dance who stood in the corner, too petrified to step anywhere near the dance floor. Maybe that's why I became a musician, so I could be in the band making the music and not on the floor dancing to it.

When I was younger, my eye contact was weak, and I stammered with a combination of unbridled enthusiasm and low self-esteem all mixed in with a good dose of attention deficit disorder. Of course, when I was a kid, A.D.D. was not a recognizably accepted label. My teachers just told me, via my report card, that I had to learn better self-control.

The simple fact was, I was bored. I would finish my work faster than the rest of my class, except, at times, for Patricia Simone. She and I used to see who could finish first and still get the higher grade. The problem was that once we were done, we would start to chat with each other as well as with our other second grade classmates who had not yet finished. That's when my self-control grades quickly descended from an S (Satisfactory) to an N (Needs Improvement) and finally landed in the basement of U (Unsatisfactory). It got so bad, that every Friday, I was forced to courier a sealed envelope, containing a note from my teacher to my parents, whose contents would determine the fate of my weekend! The Friday bus ride home was as tortuous as walking to a death sentence!

Connecting with other people was not a skill I learned until college. I started to read books like Dale Carnegie's *How to Win Friends and Influence People*, Og Mandino's *The Greatest Salesman in the World* and Tony Robbins' *Awaken the Giant* applying the practices to my interactions with everyone I met. If I was anything, I was tenacious. I would practice my newfound set of skills on friends, family, cashiers, waiters, bartenders, and eventually felt confident enough to try them with girls or more accurately by that age—women! What I learned was that I was actually likeable and less awkward than I had given myself credit for! In fact, my new skills empowered me to ask a girl out, when previously I was too intimidated to even talk with her. It was an epiphany to learn on our first date that she and others had misperceived my shyness for arrogance.

One of the most important principles I learned was that people are attracted to people who are like themselves or who are like who they want to be. When a caring adult speaks with a toddler, what do they do? They usually squat to the child's height, use shorter sentences with smaller words, or maybe even change the pitch and tempo of their voice. They're matching the child to create rapport.

This skill can be used to create rapport with anyone. If a person speaks quietly, there's less chance of creating rapport with someone who speaks loudly. If one person speaks about sports and another only speaks about politics, there is less chance that they will find each other intellectually or emotionally compatible.

When I meet a new student, I match his or her speech patterns and physical stature. When I first started using these skills, I was very conscious of matching. I actually thought that people would think I was copying them. Yet that never happened! Over the years, I've become unconsciously skilled and just do it automatically.

If my student is sitting and I need to establish rapport, I will sit; if the student is standing, I will remain standing. If the student is exuberant with his emotions, I will be more excited. If a student is more reserved, I will be more reserved. For students with whom I've had a long-term relationship, this matching occurs automatically. But it's comforting to know that when I'm not connecting with a student, I have the skills to allow me to make a better connection.

My second stage of working with a student is creating an environment of learning readiness, both internally and externally. The external environment is more easily manageable than the internal environment. The external environment is my classroom. Sure, it's the student's home, but when I walk into the home, it's no longer their home; it's my classroom. I will ask for televisions to be quieted, attention-seeking dogs to be moved to another room, disorganized books to be organized and anything else that I believe will contribute to creating the optimal external learning environment.

The other side of controlling the learning environment is assisting the student in creating an optimal *internal* learning environment. There are many things that can create internal obstacles to a student's internal learning environment. Students are impacted by many things over which neither they nor I have control. What they do have control over is how they respond to the external things that create internal blocks. I have always defined part of my job as a facilitator as providing my students with the strategies for managing their internal environment in the most effective manner conducive to learning.

My veteran students needed very little time or suggestions for managing their internal learning environments. They came to our lessons mentally prepared and able to get right into the music making. They had acquired the skills to optimally set up their internal learning environments prior to our lessons. So our lessons started right with the education of subject matter.

My 3:00 PM lesson was a high school junior with whom I had worked since she was nine. June was a responsible and accountable young lady. She was raised in a traditional Asian family who valued education and who expected the most from their children. As such, I was requested to remove my shoes when I entered their home. I always made sure that, on Monday, I didn't wear my church socks ... the ones that were "holy!"

In addition to being my first lesson of the day, her father always offered me a wonderful cup of coffee, which I gladly accepted as my energy usually hit a bit of a lull around 3:00 PM. His coffee was always perfectly brewed, and he served it with a small pitcher that held just enough cream to "tan" the coffee. I always wondered if he offered me the coffee because he sensed my lull and wanted to ensure that his daughter received a lesson with a music teacher who was fully present, or if he was just being hospitable.

We started our lesson by simply jamming on a funky blues progression, allowing her to get her fingers warmed up in a creative manner. The lesson progressed to the performance of more traditional literature she had worked on during the week.

She skillfully performed what she had practiced. The tempo was slow, but the piece was coming along.

"I like the work you did on the Gershwin Prelude this week. I'm enjoying the way it's coming together—nice smooth tempo, exciting dynamics, and rhythm."

When I looked at her, however, I saw disappointment. Her shoulders were slumped down, her eyes avoiding contact.

"You look disappointed," I said reflecting her feelings back to her.

"I didn't finish the last three lines," she replied.

"Nope, you didn't. So, what do you want to do about that? You can certainly choose to feel badly. Although, I don't quite know why you would choose that, but it's okay if you want to. My belief is that feeling badly, for *this student*," I said pointing to her and purposely using the third person "is not productive. It just puts her down. For some students to feel badly about their progress or lack thereof, is effective because it motivates them to well ... get motivated! For *this student*," I again pointed at her, "I don't believe it's productive."

What did she expect from herself? She was a high school junior taking the most challenging courses of a high school *senior* as well as playing piano in the jazz band and violin in the orchestra. Last week, she had four huge exams, a physics project, and two essays, one in political science and the other explaining Melville's use of biblical references in Moby Dick!

June had been contemplating two potential career paths—astrophysicist or music major. Ultimately, she chose the astrophysicist route. Upon first consideration, I saw these two paths as polar opposites, yet with further reflection, I comically realized that they might be more closely related than I had originally given them credit for. I have many creative musician friends who are definitely "out there." Heck, one of the drummers I know is actually nicknamed Spacey Lacey!

I noticed her shoulders shift as she sat up a little taller.

"Do you understand what I mean?" I asked.

"Yes," she said humbly.

"June, you're a wonderful young lady. What more could you have done for yourself this week? Did you put in whatever time you could?"

"Yes," she replied again, this time establishing eye contact with me.

"Then that is enough," I said.

"Music will always have a place in your life. Sometimes it will take a large role and at other times a lesser role. Presently, your main goal is creating great grades in your academic classes.

"Most likely, over the next years of your life, music will continue to take a back seat, but it will always be there for you and you for it. You have college preparations, standardized exams, college essays, then college itself and then a job and career all ahead of you. It's not okay for me if you continue to feel guilty about not progressing at a quick pace in music. You're a *wonderful* young musician and young lady.

"You're an awesome young jazz pianist. You have a strong foundation of classical music from every genre. You compose and play pop music with your sister. You play violin in the pit orchestra of your high school musical. You're well equipped to do anything you want with *your* music. One of the things I would prefer, is if you wouldn't beat yourself up about what you didn't accomplish. It's all about balance. And balance is dynamic; it's always changing based upon what else is happening in life."

"But I made a commitment to practice more this week. I fell short of my commitment."

"June, life isn't just one big commitment. It's more of a series of constant recommitments. People start a diet, then go off it, then recommit and start again. People work out, then stop, then recommit and start again. People decide to stop smoking and then have a cigarette, then recommit and decide to quit again. Life is just a string of recommitments. Once you recognize you are off course, just make an adjustment to restore the balance and recommit."

She was smiling. "Got it," she said as she nodded her head. "Thank you," she continued.

"You're welcome," I said with a smile.

Sometimes people just need to be reminded that they're simply complete and good enough just as they are, doing whatever it is they're doing.

The moments that my job aligns with my mission of providing an environment where people are empowered to create feelings of pride and live to actualize their fullest potential of happiness are wonderful. Today, my mission was accomplished.

CHAPTER 13

If it wasn't for the weekly countdown of ensuring that each of NOTES: my students had a holiday song to perform for their families, Christmas would've just snuck up on me with the stealth of a lion hunting its prey.

Diane's Christmas gift to me was a new ski jacket and ski gloves. My gift to her was a weekend at a Vermont bed and breakfast called the Seven Gables Inn. Skiing was one of the things on my bucket list. I had booked the ski trip for the weekend of January 5th.

On Thursday morning, January 5th, we packed our bags and drove for six hours to the Seven Gables Inn. The inn was very low key, run by a couple who had transplanted to Vermont from New York City in an effort to lead a calmer, scaled-down life. It seemed to me that they actually worked pretty hard for people who wanted to scale down, but they seemed content and were very gracious hosts.

Diane and I were tired from the six-hour drive and, in preparation for an early start to tomorrow's day of skiing, went to bed early.

At 7:30 the next morning, we awoke to the smell of bacon, freshly made muffins, and my absolutely favorite morning scent—a strong brew of coffee. Diane ordered a basket of assorted homemade muffins and scones. She was forever in search of the perfect scone, as I was for the perfect pizza. Since pizza was not on the menu, I ordered stuffed French toast.

The French toast was simply incredible with that stick-to-your-ribs quality needed before venturing out in seven-degree weather. It was stuffed with a mixture of cream cheese, molasses, walnuts, and raisins and topped with warm Vermont maple syrup. I don't know if it was called *stuffed* because the toast was stuffed or because that's how you felt after eating just one of the four pieces you were given. The only thing I wanted to do after eating it was to go back to bed and work on my impression of a bear in hibernation. Around 8:30, we drove three miles to the ski lodge to get our gear.

The beginning of the day was spent with Diane trying to teach me to ski. This was semi-successful. I was fine as long as no one had fallen in front of me, and I was facing in a downward direction. Otherwise, Diane was picking me out of groups of other fallen skiers or out of the wooded areas that banked the trails.

I spent the first two hours attempting to learn how to ski by trusting my natural skiing "instincts." What I learned was that skiing was hard (as was the soft, fluffy white stuff) and my instincts for skiing were basically non-existent. I was looking forward to taking my skiing lesson after lunch.

We broke for lunch around 11:30, which quickly became my favorite part of this *adventure* (as Diane tried to reframe it for me). Following lunch, the only thing I wanted to do was to proceed to before-dinner cocktails, or what the ski community had named aprés ski but, apparently, 12:30 was too early for this event to begin.

My skiing lesson was scheduled for 1:00. While I met with my instructor, Colin, Diane went out to ski the intermediate and advance slopes. Colin introduced himself with a toothy smile, removed his glove, and extended his arm to shake my hand. "Hi! You must be Matt. I'm Colin."

It had taken me quite a while, after lunch, to get my gloves back on, working the inner layer on one finger at a time, and there was little chance of me actually taking off my glove and shaking Colin's hand in an appropriate gentlemanly way. So, I just raised my gloved hand in a wave and said, "Hi, Colin. Yes, I'm Matt."

Colin was probably fresh out of high school. It looked like he shaved once a week, cheeks a healthy glow of red from the cold. The hair that stuck out from the sides of his purple and yellow ski cap was blonde, which made me think that Colin should be surfing somewhere.

"So, how long have you been skiing?" Colin asked.

I looked up at the sun, estimated the time, and said, "About four hours and fifteen minutes, minus thirty minutes for lunch."

"Oh, so you're probably ready for the black diamonds run!" Colin replied.

"Hardly. The only diamonds I'm interested in at this point, are on a baseball field."

"Okay, so what have you been doing?" Colin asked.

"Mostly running into other fallen skiers and trying not to look like a fool in front of my girlfriend, which appear to be mutually exclusive goals."

Colin laughed. "Well, let's fix that!" he said with the enthusiasm I was lacking.

"Let's hop on the lift that goes to the top of the Green slope," Colin suggested.

Because Colin was an instructor, we moved to the beginning of the line and immediately boarded our departing chair.

On the way up, I found out that my instincts weren't off. Colin was, in fact, a surfer as well as a skier and snowboarder. In the summer months, he flew back home to the west coast and taught surfing. When he wasn't surfing, he was teaching snowboarding in Vail. He was only in Vermont visiting a friend for a few weeks and decided to pick up a little extra cash by giving skiing lessons.

Colin asked me about my career, and I told him I showed people how to grow as people while learning the piano.

"So, you're a piano teacher?" he offered.

"Not exactly, I'm an educator who teaches people the language of music through the piano."

"Sounds interesting," Colin replied as he smiled politely while pondering my abbreviated elevator sales pitch.

"So, how long have you been skiing?" I asked.

"As long as I can remember. I put myself through college by teaching skiing. My parents were instructors at a local ski academy where I grew up in Colorado. So I've had skis on my feet since the day I could walk. I guess that makes it twenty-one years. Come to think of it, I don't ever remember even being taught; I just skied."

Suddenly I wondered if Colin was the right teacher for me. If he had never struggled to learn how to ski, how would he know how I felt?

The chair reached the top of the lift; I exited and quickly skied directly into a group of beginner skiers who, just like me, could not negotiate the left-handed turn at the exit of the lift.

Colin came over to me, helped me up, and pointed me in the correct direction. "Let's see what you've got!" he exclaimed with way too much excitement for my fragile ego.

I started my descent and progressed about thirty yards before once again crashing into another fallen skier, but not before I had gained a considerable amount of speed.

After I apologized to the skier with whom I had collided as well as for the frantic screaming and arm flailing which had preceded the collision, Colin once again righted me and pointed me downward. As I started my second descent, the trail turned in a wide arch to my right, but my skis did not, they continued in a perfectly straight line—directly into the woods.

Colin collected my ski poles (why they gave beginner skiers these weapons was a mystery to me!), plucked me out of the woods, and smiled. "I know how to fix your problem, and it's easy!"

Once again, that damned enthusiasm of someone who "just skied."

"Great. How?" I said despondently.

"Only look where you want to go," he said.

"Excuse me? Can you expand on that a bit?"

"Only look where you want to go. You keep seeing the obstacles, instead of the path," he reiterated.

"Look, let's start down the mountain again and let me coach you. I'll be your 'inner skiing voice.' All you have to do is listen and respond," Colin said.

"Okay," I replied sheepishly.

Colin righted me and pointed me in the direction of the turn; I started to move down the mountain. Just as I was heading into the wooded area on the other side of the trail, I heard Colin's voice from behind me, "Where do you want to go?"

I pointed left across the trail and, like magic, my skis turned, and I was once again facing a clear run!

As I was mentally celebrating this minor success, I saw a fallen skier directly in my path and once again heard Colin's voice, "Where do you want to go?"

I pointed left and once again, like magic, my skis followed and I avoided the fallen skier.

Colin continued to be my "skiing GPS" the rest of the way down the slope and, to my surprise, I reached the bottom without ever feeling the ground on *my* bottom.

When I stopped (using the children's method of making a pizza slice with my skis—pizza seemed to be a running theme in my life), I was all smiles.

"Wow! That was my first time making it down the entire slope without falling!" I exclaimed.

"Yep, skiing is simple. Only look where you want to go," Colin replied.

"Do you want to do it again? There are still thirty minutes left on your lesson," Colin asked.

"No. That's just the right amount of information for me. I think I can manage on my own! You can go on to your next lesson," I replied.

"Okay. Good luck and enjoy the rest of your day," Colin said with his characteristic enthusiasm.

I skied for the next twenty minutes by myself and fully enjoyed the peacefulness of gliding down the plush white carpet that covered the mountain.

Diane and I met up again at the chair lift for the beginner slope, and she asked me how my lesson had gone.

"Great! I don't know if the instructor knew the impact of what he was saying, but his instruction was apropos to both skiing and life."

Diane looked at me with widened eyes and said, "You just can't take something at face value; you always have to find a life lesson in it, don't you?"

"No. There really was a life lesson." I pushed back.

"Okay. What were these great words of wisdom imparted to you by a simple ski instructor?" she asked with sarcasm.

"What he said was, 'Only look where you want to go,'" I replied.

"Only look where you want to go?" Diane repeated.

"Yes."

"And those are words of both skiing and life wisdom?" she taunted.

"Absolutely. Think about it. Don't see the obstacles, just the path. When I focused on the obstacles on the ski slope, I usually ran right into them. Yet, when I focused on the path I wanted to travel, I simply went around the obstacles without even considering them. It's just like Ray asking me 'What do you want?'"

"Okay, I see what you mean. Do you want to demonstrate your newly found philosophy for me on the ski slope?" she teased.

"Let's go!"

I loved learning new information that applied to my life and the lives of my students, things that seemed so innocuous yet, upon further inspection, had much deeper meanings. They provided me with an arsenal of metaphors for connecting with my students and were important lessons for me as well. I couldn't wait to have the opportunity to share this one! "Only look where you want to go!"

CHAPTER 14

February was a jumble of snowed-out piano lessons that needed to be rescheduled. It felt as if there was at least one considerable snowfall each week and lessons were cancelled because the roads were bad or my clients had lost power. I taught make-up lessons almost every Saturday in order to cover the lessons that had been cancelled.

March arrived and the annual tug-of-war between winter and spring started. On March 10th, spring scored a major victory as it almost appeared that the early days of summer had come to its rescue. The temperature soared to a warm and welcome seventy degrees. Adults responded by putting the tops down on their cars and children responded by putting aside their iParaphernalia and taking out their bikes, skateboards, and roller blades.

When I arrived at my first student's home, he was outside with his brother. They were playing with a magnifying glass.

"Wow, that's a cool magnifying glass. Where did you get it?" I asked Max, my student.

"We were at my pop-pops this weekend and he gave it to us. It was in his office."

The magnifying glass was about four inches in diameter, surrounded by a brass ring with a handle made from what appeared to be a deer antler.

"Pop-Pop said that the handle was made from the antler of a deer that his father killed with a bow and arrow," Max said with pride.

"What are you looking at with it?" I asked as the boys inspected different objects in the yard.

"Just different stuff," said Tyler, Max's brother.

"Did you know that a magnifying glass can be used to start a fire if the sun's light is focused correctly?" I asked the boys.

They both looked at me, wondering if I was serious. After all, last summer I had told their younger brother, Kevin, that his Cheerios were donut seeds.

Kevin was four and had come into our lesson with a bag of Cheerios. I asked him what he was eating. "O's," was his monosyllabic reply.

"Those aren't O's," I replied.

"Yes, they are," Kevin said matter-of-factly.

"No, they're not," I said.

"Then what are they?" he challenged with a furrowed brow and pursed lips.

"Those are donut seeds. If you plant them in your backyard and water them every day, you'll get a donut tree. Your mom got you the plain ones, so you'll just get plain donuts, but if she had gotten you the chocolate ones, you would get chocolate donuts from the tree."

I came back the following week and Kevin's mom, Sue, asked me what I had told Kevin last week. To be candid, I really didn't remember, I tell lots of kids lots of stuff each week!

"I'm not sure what you're referring to," I replied.

"Well, shortly after you left the lesson, Kevin went into our backyard and planted his Cheerios in the garden. He's been watering them every day since."

It was all I could do to keep from falling over with laughter! Had I known he was going to do this, I might have bought some plain donuts, stuck a twig in the ground, and hung the donuts on the branches!

I explained to Sue what I had told Kevin and she was hysterical. Good thing she had a sense of humor!

So, it wasn't surprising that Max and Tyler didn't believe me about the sun and the magnifying glass. I wasn't sure I should be telling a ten-year-old and his eight-year-old brother how to light stuff on fire with the assistance of a magnifying glass.

As I was contemplating the prudence of my words and how to potentially back out with dignity, Sue appeared at the front door. "Hi Matt! What a beautiful day!"

"Hi Sue. The boys were just showing me the magnifying glass their pop-pop gave them."

"They haven't stopped using it since Saturday when we visited my parents."

I saw my way out of the pickle I had put myself in. "Is it okay if I show them how the sun can get really hot if they use the magnifying glass the right way?"

"You mean like burning a piece of paper like we used to do when we were kids?" she replied.

"Exactly," I said.

"Sure, as long as they know that they shouldn't do that without an adult around and that they need to be very careful," she replied loud enough so that her sons could hear her.

She looked at Max and Tyler and, with a raised eyebrow asked, "Do you two understand?"

"Yes, Mom," the boys replied excitedly.

"Sure, that will be fine, Matt. Thanks for asking," Sue said.

We found a leaf that was dry and first I showed them how the sun could just shine light on the leaf, like a giant spotlight. Then, I showed them how, by tipping the magnifying glass at a different angle, the rays of the sun could be intensified so much that they could burn a hole through the leaf.

"Wow! That's awesome!" Max exclaimed, my coolness factor moving up a notch in his mind. I was about to bring it back down to adult reality.

"Remember what you told your mom? You really can get into trouble if you light something on fire, so only do this with an adult around. Promise?"

"Yes," they said in a unified voice of compliance. Because they were respectful, rule-following kids, I believed them.

"Now, let's go inside and have your piano lesson, Max."

Max stood up, picked up the leaf and looked through the small hole I had made. He carried the magnifying glass with him into the lesson.

When Max sat at the piano, he placed the magnifying glass on the bench next to him.

"So, what was your proudest accomplishment at the piano this week?" I asked.

"I can play my recital piece really fast!" Max said, enthusiastically.

"Great. Are you ready to show me now, or do you want to warm up first?" I asked.

"Nope. I'm warm from being outside in the sun. I can just play it," Max replied.

He played the piece very quickly (all kids love to play fast), but it was clear that, like the majority of kids, Max hadn't practice the piece in small sections. His practicing clearly consisted of having reviewed the song by playing it from beginning to end. The mistakes he made last week were still there; they were just harder to hear because he played through them faster.

I didn't want to create a feeling for him that destroyed the pride he had in playing it fast. He clearly had practiced, but he hadn't practiced with the correct goal.

Practicing anything always yields an ability to reproduce what is practiced. We're always learning. We just have to be conscious of what we're learning. We could be learning how to do something correctly or incorrectly. Either way, we're learning, so I couldn't accuse him of not learning. Max had learned; he had learned how to play his mistakes even quicker than before!

I had to show him how to get more out of his practicing, how to foc ....

"Max, it's clear that you spent a lot of time on that this week. You can play it a lot faster than you did last week! I'm proud of you and that you made the time to practice."

"Thanks!" Max replied, nodding his head with pride.

"What would you say if I could show you how to get even better results with *less* practice time?" I asked, baiting him a bit.

"That would be cool."

I picked up the magnifying glass. "Remember before when we used this to just shine a bright spotlight on the leaf?"

"Yeah, but burning a hole through it was really cool!" Max predictably replied. Bait taken—hook line and sinker!

"Exactly. When you focus the sun's rays of light and energy properly, it's even more powerful than just *shining* its light. That's exactly how you get more out of your practice. You focus *your own mental rays of energy*. Like the sun, if we just put the rays all over the leaf it makes the leaf warm, but the rays aren't powerful enough to burn through the leaf. Well, when you practice, if you play from the beginning to the end and then again from the beginning to the end and you keep doing this, it makes the piece nice and 'warm,' but it never really 'burns a hole' through the challenging parts.

"Do you hear those spots where the piece stumbles?" I asked, purposely not asking "where he stumbles" so that he could be more objective.

"Yes, between the third and fourth lines," Max replied.

"Yep, that's where I hear it too. Excellent job identifying a tough spot," I said validating him.

"Well, instead of just warming the piece up each time you practice it, how about if we just burn a hole through that section by only practicing from the end of the third line into the fourth line? This way you'll be focusing your practicing energy better."

"You mean don't play the whole piece?" Max asked with concern.

"That's correct. Just focus your energy on that one spot."

"Okay, I can try that," Max said.

I sat back and let him give it a whirl. He was an excellent problem solver, having mastered many important learning strategies to conquer a challenge.

"Can I try it with each hand separately first?"

"Sure. That sounds like a great idea."

"Can I slow it down?"

"If it helps you focus your energy and master this part, certainly!" I encouraged.

He continued to work for about six minutes before he played it through accurately.

"Hey, I got it!" Max exclaimed.

"Yep, great job. I like the way you used different ideas to make the challenge more accomplishable. You tried separate hands, and you slowed the tempo down. That's awesome," I continued to encourage.

"Can I try it from the beginning?" Max asked.

"If you think you've 'burned through' the obstacle connecting lines three to four, sure," I replied.

Max played the song from the beginning and once again stumbled through the connection between lines three and four.

He looked at me disappointed. "I thought I had it. I did it before," he said a bit dejected.

"Max, let me ask you something. If you do something wrong ten times and then you do it right one time, which way are you better at doing it, wrong or right?"

"Wrong," Max said.

"That's correct. So, for the past three weeks you played through this section without really working it out super accurately. Now you've decided not to accept the sections that didn't sound as smooth as the rest. You worked on that section for six or seven minutes and got it right. You got it right once, but you had played it inaccurately many more times!"

"Oh, so once I get it right I have to keep playing it, until I can do it a lot more times right than wrong?"

"Now you've got it!" I was impressed by how quickly he caught on.

Max smiled, turned to the piano and worked on that spot for another several minutes before I asked him if he understood how to practice this piece.

"You know what would be a good reminder for me, Mr. Matt?" he asked.

"What's that, Max?"

"How about if I keep Pop-Pop's magnifying glass with me when I practice so I can remember to focus on the challenging parts?"

"That sounds like a great idea, Max! I like the way you think. Hey, why don't we call it a *max*-ifying glass because your name is Max and when you use it you maximize your practicing by being more focused?"

"That's cool! I have a *max*-ifying glass."

"What do you think about going through your piece and writing down each specific area that you want to use your *max*-ifying glass on this week?"

"Yeah, that would help me so that when I practice I don't have to keep playing the whole piece each day."

He took out his weekly goal book and wrote down each challenge, line-by-line, measure-by-measure. His list included five specific areas.

"I really think this will help and all because of my pop-pop's magnifying ... I mean *max*-ifying glass!"

CHAPTER 15

It was Monday morning, and I was working in my office NOTES: dispersing the money I had made to others who had provided me with services. Some people call this *paying bills* I call it spreading the wealth. I had read somewhere that that's why money is called currency, because it must flow, like a current. I was lost in my thoughts when my business phone rang. One of my student's numbers appeared on the caller ID.

"Hello, Higher Ground Music."

"Hi Matt. It's Stephen Gantz, Jared's father."

Stephen was a businessman who did a lot of traveling, both in and out of the country. From what I had gathered in my conversations with his son, in addition to English, he spoke three languages fluently—Farsi, Mandarin, and German—and could calculate numbers faster than you could enter them in a calculator. He was the founder and CEO of Gantz Imports and was able to secure huge deals where others had failed. He had a way of appearing very simple and laid-back, your "Average Joe" type of guy. When in reality, his intelligence was far beyond average and he was quick to accurately size up a situation and find out how he could benefit from it. He was a formidable businessman.

Stephen and I had had very few interactions, as he was usually traveling when I saw Jared for his lessons. Once, however, I had rescheduled Jared's lesson for a Saturday morning and Stephen was home. After the lesson, he complimented me on how I "handled" his son. He said that I appeared very kind on the outside, but it was clear my kindness wasn't softness, as I didn't buy into his son's excuses for lack of progress. He liked the fact that I wasn't demeaning to Jared but still held him accountable. He said, "You have a special way with kids." I thought his quick, armchair evaluation of my educational philosophy was insightful and was happy to have been recognized for more than just being someone who taught notes, rhythms, and hand positions.

I had been working with his son for the past five years. Usually, when Jared, a high school senior, had to change his lesson time, he would call, so it was odd to hear from Stephen. Hmm, he was on several community boards, maybe he wanted me to donate some lessons to a local raffle.

Jared was a good kid, a straight A student. His demeanor was of a low profile kid. Yet I always sensed that his exterior austerity was a curtain to a profusion of activity going on inside of his being. I guess the best way to describe it is to say that at times, he felt "heavy" to me. He also tended to gravitate to music that was darker in nature.

"Hi, Stephen. What's up?"

"This is a bit awkward for me, so I'll just get to the point." (Stephen the businessman appeared to be speaking.) "Jared admitted himself to the hospital. He said he was having thoughts of hurting himself. He's in the psyche ward at North Shore General."

Whoa! Psyche ward? Admitted himself? Hurt himself? What was Stephen talking about?

There was an extended silence on the phone as I processed what was just shared with me.

"Stephen, forgive my silence, but I'm speechless."

"I understand, he's my son, and I'm speechless. So I know how you feel."

"Can you share any more with me?"

"Jared admitted himself on Saturday night. He was supposed to go to a party; Cathy and I were out at a business function when we got the call from the hospital. Jared had called a crisis hotline. The counselor on the line spoke with him while a mobile crisis unit was dispatched to our home. The mobile unit took him to North Shore."

"Please forgive my directness, but is 'thoughts of hurting himself' a euphemism for committing suicide?"

"No forgiveness necessary. Your directness with Jared is one of the things I have always respected about you. In response to your question, yes, I believe that is the hospital's way of not creating panic.

"I'm sure you know that Jared writes in his journal on a daily basis. Well, he shared with me that he was rereading his journal entries of the past week and saw a consistent gloom to his thoughts that he didn't like. He wasn't comfortable with what he was reading and decided to reach out to the hotline."

"I'm glad he felt healthy enough to recognize that he wasn't having healthy thoughts and was able to reach out for help," I replied.

"Yes, for that, Cathy and I feel blessed.

"The reason I called, however, is because Jared was permitted to make a short list of people he wanted to see while he was in the hospital. He listed his four immediate family members, one uncle, one aunt … and you."

Me? I was *just* his piano teacher. While I never really viewed myself as just a piano teacher, this was more than I bargained for. *Be careful what you wish for; you may just get it.*

"I'm calling you to see if you would be comfortable visiting Jared."

My response wasn't thought out; it was simply a "knee-jerk" reaction. "Certainly. When is he in the hospital until?"

"As I said, he admitted himself on Saturday and we expect that he will stay the week."

"When are visiting hours?"

"Every day from 12 – 8:30 PM. In the mornings, he is in sessions with a doctor and a small group."

"Yes, I will definitely make the time to see him. Should I call first?"

"Actually, I think that his doctor would prefer that he calls you. He is permitted phone time after his group session."

"That's fine. Please give him my cell number."

"Thank you. Matt, you hold a very high place in Jared's life. You are so much more than a piano teacher to him. You are a role model and a confidant. He feels very comfortable talking with you." Stephen's speech had become strained. He abruptly paused and cleared his throat. "I'm not sure how to express my gratitude as a father, except to say 'Thank you' in a way that is so beyond what those words can express. Thank you."

I wanted to say, "No problem," or "Don't mention it," but one knee-jerk reaction today was enough. Instead, I responded with, "You're welcome."

Sometimes people have a difficult time accepting the purity and value to a heartfelt "Thank you." They stumble with comments, "Don't worry about it," "No problem," "Don't mention it," when the only appropriate response is a humble "You're welcome." Accepting the fact that someone received value from something you have done or who you are is sobering. I was deeply appreciative and honored.

I gave Stephen my cell number, hung up the phone, and sat in reflective silence.

Over the past several weeks, Jared and I had done less piano playing and more conversing about life. That wasn't an uncommon occurrence with my graduating seniors. Some people saw this as a waste of time. I didn't. Part of my job was to create an environment in which learning could occur. If there were blocks to this environment, I tried, to the best of my ability—as I am not a therapist or a counselor—to either sidestep them or work through them with the student. I now realized, it was the "create" part of my three-part educational blueprint.

Lately, Jared had shared with me about his relationship with one of his friends who was a girl. When I asked him if it was his girlfriend, he said, "No, we're friends with benefits."

"Friends with benefits?" I replied. "I don't understand. Do you mean she has health insurance and retirement plans?"

He just looked at me with an uncomfortable grin. I wasn't sure if the uncomfortable part was because he knew I was teasing him about the benefits or if it was because, at the young age of seventeen, he had no idea that health insurance and retirement plans were called benefits!

I knew what he was speaking about, but had never heard the term that this generation used for it. Friends with benefits! I wondered if things were okay with this girl, or if this was part of the problem that caused Jared to admit himself to the hospital. I knew that this was his first relationship and, without the appropriate skills, he might not know how to handle the emotional intensity of it.

Jared also shared some of his poetry with me, which, like the music he listened to, was dark. It was incredibly well written and made some wonderfully insightful points but, after reading it, I felt, well ... heavy and disturbed.

Nothing, however, in the poetry suggested that I needed to alert his parents. I tell students who begin to confide in me that I will keep our conversations confidential unless I feel that their physical or emotional safety is at risk, in which case I am obligated to speak with their parents. So Jared's father's phone call was a bit uprooting for me.

Students, for some reason, find it easy to talk to me. A student once said, "Mr. Matt, you would be a great psychologist. It's much easier to talk with you than it is with my therapist!" I explained to her that, first, I am not a counselor, therapist, or psychologist and second that the reason she found it easier to talk with me was *because* I wasn't her counselor, therapist, or psychologist; I was *just* her piano teacher. She replied, "Actually, you're a success coach disguised as a piano teacher!" That felt like a big hat to wear, but maybe it would fit.

In the silence, I continued to reflect on Jared. Did I miss some signals? No, I don't believe I did. Was I present enough in our lessons to be aware of any potential dangers? Yes, I'm always present when I'm working with my students.

At 12:15, my cell phone rang. It was Diane asking if I wanted to have lunch together.

I didn't want Jared's call to go to voice mail, so I was abrupt with her.

"I'm not sure, but I can't get into it right now. I need to keep off my cell phone. I'm expecting an important call. I'll call you back."

"Are you okay?"

"Yes, I'm fine, but I can't get into it right now. I have to keep my cell open. I'll call you in a bit."

"Okay. Goodbye."

I'm glad I got off the phone quickly, because less than half a minute later, it rang again. This time it was a call from the hospital. I know because I recognized the exchange from a little over a year ago when my dad was in for bypass surgery. He had had complications with the surgery and was in the hospital for several days. The calls to the hospital, three times a day, had the exchange embedded in my brain—669.

"Hello."

"Hi, Matt, it's Jared. My dad gave me your number."

Jared sounded understandably cautious.

"Hi, Jared. How are you doing?" I wasn't quite sure of a comfortable way to get the conversation started. Jared took care of that.

"My dad told me he shared with you that I admitted myself."

"Yes, he did."

"The hospital asked me to create a small list of people who I would want to visit me. I hope it was okay that I put your name on the list."

There was no knee-jerk reaction for me this time. I was in teacher mode and acted appropriately. For some reason when I put on my "teacher hat," I thought and acted differently. Like Clarke Kent putting on his Superman outfit, I transformed. I expected—no that's not quite right—I knew the right answers would come out of my mouth. I should probably wear my "teacher hat" all the time.

"Jared, why wouldn't it be okay? It's your list," I responded.

"I guess you're right," he replied.

"If you're not too busy, it would be good to see you," he continued.

"Well considering that our lesson on Tuesdays is my last lesson of the day, why don't we have your lesson in your hospital room?" I asked with a light touch of sarcasm.

Well versed in the language of sarcasm, Jared replied, "Well I'll have to see if they can get a piano here and, honestly, I haven't made much time to practice."

I laughed, "Sure. I'll make the time to come and see you. How about tomorrow night at 7:30?"

"Visiting hours end at 8:30, so 7:30 would be good."

"Great. I'll see you then."

Just in case there was something else he wanted to share, I waited for Jared to hang up the phone. There wasn't, and I sat with an empty phone line to my ear for a few moments.

I called Diane back, apologized for my abruptness, and let her know that one of my students had admitted himself to the psyche ward of North Shore Community hospital and that he had asked to see me.

"When are you going to see him?"

"Tomorrow."

CHAPTER 16

My last lesson on Tuesday ended at a little after seven. I had NOTES: about ten minutes to get myself something to eat before I was to meet with Jared. I stopped at a local pizzeria for a couple of slices and a Diet Coke. There's something very gratifying about eating pizza at a pizzeria. The ovens embrace you with their warmth, there's the delicious smell of garlic and olive oil, you can see the bubbling of the pie, and you can hear the scrape of the pizza pies being deposited and removed from the oven. It all equates to an experience that take-out cannot match.

I stepped up to the counter and I was greeted by a high school girl and a sign. The girl welcomed me and asked what I wanted; the sign welcomed me and told me that the servers would be happy to take my order as long as I was not having a conversation on a cell phone. Excellent. One of the pet peeves I had developed, as technology continued its infiltration of human life, was trying to talk with someone who was already talking with someone! You wouldn't even consider having two entirely different conversations with two people in person, so why would you do it with a cyber-person and a live person? I think I had found a pizzeria I would return to … as long as the pizza was good.

"Love your sign," I said to the girl behind the counter.

"The owner is an older Italian man, and he simply refuses to serve anyone who's talking to us while on a cell phone. He's actually from Italy where 'Eating is its own event, not something that connects other events in life,' so he says. One of my friends actually lost her job here because a couple of times she didn't enforce his rule! It really bothers him."

"I understand and completely get where he's coming from. I'm glad to see this in today's fast-paced world. Can I have two slices and a Diet Coke please? You can just make the slices warm as I don't have too much time."

"A pie just came out of the oven. That'll be $6.50 please."

As she reached for my slices and Diet Coke, I placed a five-dollar bill and six quarters on the counter.

"Hmm, that smells great. Thank you," I said.

"You're welcome."

I took a seat at a table for two and, in contrast to the leisurely style of Italian dining, consumed the slices American style—a couple of quick bites, a few sips of the Diet Coke to wash the slices down, and I was off.

I pulled my car into the parking garage of the hospital, took my parking ticket from the meter, and walked across the enclosed crosswalk. The snow flurry predicted for 8:00 PM had arrived early, and I appreciated the warmth of the enclosure. Spring was yet to have the last word. The crosswalk led me to the main lobby where I walked up to the front desk to get a pass.

"Can I help you?" a woman of about sixty asked.

"Hello. Yes, I'm here to visit Jared Gantz," I replied.

The woman searched her computer, reached into a file cabinet to her left and pulled out a yellow pass.

"Sixth floor, room 649. The elevators are on your left down that hallway," she said as she pointed to her right.

"Thank you."

"You're welcome."

I walked to the elevator, pressed the *up* button, and waited. I waited about a minute and even though the *up* button was still lit, I pressed it again. I guess the only thing that did was to give me something to do to satiate my impatience! That'll show all those people who think I'm patient.

The elevator arrived about five seconds after my second button push, and I righteously told myself that it was the second push that expedited its delivery.

I stepped in, hit the *number six* button twice (hey, it worked on the *up* button) and was promptly delivered to the sixth floor. Upon stepping out of the elevator, a sign directed me to go left for rooms 610-650 and right for rooms 651-675. I didn't really think it mattered since the hospital was shaped in a circle, but I obediently followed directions and went left.

A nurse's station was central to the wrap-around hallway. When I arrived at Jared's room, he was reading.

"Hi, Matt! Thanks for coming by."

"Not a challenge. How are you doing?" I asked as I took off my coat and hat and hung them on a hanger in the open closet to my right.

"Okay, I guess," Jared replied.

As we looked at each other, there was silence. Jared's eye contact was better but he was clearly uncomfortable with the connection.

"I'm glad your dad contacted me," I stated.

"I asked him to," Jared replied.

"So, what's going on? What motivated you to take the action you did?"

"Well, my parents were out on Saturday night, and I was supposed to see my friend, but she called me at the last minute to cancel because she was going out with some other friends."

"Is this the 'friend with a retirement plan' girl?" I asked to both be clear and to lighten the heaviness I was starting to feel in the room, but probably more to lighten the heaviness. What did I expect, a Disney movie? This was a heavy topic, someone's life, the life of one of my students. I guess I didn't adequately emotionally prepare myself for seeing him, but this was an event that was out of my comfort zone. I had no way of knowing how I was going to feel when I saw him because I had never visited a student who had put himself on suicide watch.

"Yes, my 'friend with benefits.' Her name is Julie," he replied without emotion.

"Okay, I just wanted to keep things straight."

Sometimes, interrupting to clarify is good; sometimes it's not. Clarifying when a person is sharing factual information—like meeting times and agendas, insurance plan terms, or warranty information—is good. Clarifying when someone is sharing his or her feelings creates blocks and prevents continuity for the sharer.

When someone is sharing feelings, it's best to just listen and provide an occasional nod of encouragement for the person to continue. I wouldn't interrupt him again until he either asked me a question or was finished. I sat back in my chair, intertwined my fingers, relaxed my mind and face, and just listened.

Jared continued, "When Julie texted me to tell me we weren't getting together, I felt very disappointed. To be honest with you, I was, well, excited about seeing her, because we would have had a chance to be alone as my parents and sister wouldn't be home."

"We texted back and forth a bit with me trying to convince her to come over. One of the guys from the lacrosse team was having a party and she was going with her friends. She didn't invite me, so I felt left out.

"With nothing else to do, I started to write and draw in my journal. The entry was, at first, just me blowing off some steam, but then my mood shifted. I started to think about all the things in my life that disappointed me—some of my recent grades, my stagnation at the piano, my parent's relationship, my trepidation about which college I was going to choose, who I was going to the prom with, if I was even going to go the prom, and my confusion as to whether I'm gay or straight."

It's no wonder his mood had shifted, I was starting to feel overwhelmed just listening to him.

"I started rereading some of my previous entries. I began thinking about if the world would be a better place without me in it. Really, what good was I doing anyway? My dad always told me I was underachieving, 'not living up to my potential' he would say. My mom was always off to pageants with my sister. I mean she was the star of the family.

"I started to consider how I would like to die. I don't do drugs, so I didn't think that would work. Plus, I didn't know any drug dealers or where to find them, and I'm petrified of needles. Then I thought about a bad car accident, but one, I didn't want to hurt someone else and two, well, all the cars in the house were out.

"Then I thought about hanging myself but wasn't sure how to tie the knots and, when I thought about tying the knots, I started to consider something you once said about me overthinking things and 'tying my brain in knots.' I started to feel like I couldn't breathe, and I was completely overwhelmed by darkness and heaviness.

"It reminded me of a vacation my family and I went on when I was younger. We took a boat tour of a cavern. It was ninety feet below the surface of the earth. At one point, the guide shut off his guide light and asked us to remain perfectly still and silent. It was insanely dark and quiet! I remember feeling my heartbeat starting to speed up and actually hearing it in my ears! It was a silence and darkness I had never experienced.

"The guide told us that if we were stuck down here with no light for just one month we would go blind because our pupils, in an effort to get any available light into our eyes, would dilate so much that they would paralyze themselves open. Some people might find the dark and quiet peaceful; I found it petrifying! I just kept thinking about what I would do if I somehow got stuck in a cavern. I wouldn't know which way was out or where safety was. I started to think how, no matter how much I screamed, no one would hear me, and I would just die down there.

"Then something else you had once said to me in one of our lessons screamed in my ear."

I waited, a bit in shock that I had said something that was powerful enough for him to remember in such a time of crisis, and also because I didn't want to block him from continuing. Apparently, he wanted me to interact with him.

"Do you know what it was?" Jared asked.

"Well, I've said a lot of things to you. Do you want me to guess?" I replied.

"Sure," he said with a little smile and a nod.

"The skiing story about focusing on what you wanted and where you wanted to go, not on what you feared?" I asked.

"Yep, that was it. What I wanted was to feel safe and clear. That's when I decided to call a crisis help line. The woman who answered the phone was named Faith. I immediately saw that as a sign. I didn't know if anyone at the center was really named Faith or Hope, but it worked for me. We spoke for a while and she said that she was sending a mobile crisis vehicle to my home. We continued speaking and about ten minutes later a car arrived. The young man who came to my door told me he was from North Shore General. We spoke for about five minutes and then he asked me to go to the hospital with him."

"As you were telling me about all of the problems you were thinking about, *I* was starting to feel down. I can easily see how that thought process would quickly throw you into an unwanted mental state. Your mind is an incredible tool. You can use it to create fear-invoking thoughts that immobilize you or inspiring thoughts that motivate you to succeed. Many people just allow their minds to go on autopilot instead of directing or choosing what to think about. The thoughts you plant in your mind will either grow to be beautiful flowers or ugly weeds."

"The social worker that conducts the morning group says the exact same thing! He's a really great guy named Gene," Jared interjected.

"Gene says, 'Focus on what you want, not on what you fear, because whatever you continuously focus on becomes your reality.'

"Each morning we make a list of what we want and carry that with us to read throughout the day and especially every time we start to feel overwhelmed by those scary thoughts. Gene says he likes to keep things simple, because it's not uncommon for people like me to get into a spiraling pattern of negative thinking. It's just a matter of consistently refocusing on what I want. Sometimes I have to do that minute by minute."

"I understand. So, what do you want?"

"I want all of my problems to go away, but I know that's not possible," he said with a small smile.

"I want to feel clear about what I want. To be honest with you, I don't really know what I want. I know what other people expect of me, you know, college and success and stuff, but I don't know if that's what *I* want.

"I'm feeling more hopeful. I don't know if it's the talks or being out of my home environment, or the fact that everyone, including my family, is so compassionate."

"It's probably a combination of all the things you mentioned. Is your family in counseling also?"

"Yes, it's a requirement to be part of the program in this hospital.

"My dad is an excellent provider, but one of the problems of his business success is that I rarely see him. He's always traveling. Last year, he was on the road for 290 days! I'd rather live in a less luxurious house and have him home more. I understand why he needs to be so successful, so that helps a bit," Jared continued.

"What do you mean by 'needs to be'?" I asked.

"My dad was really poor when he was a child. My grandfather was a laborer who was out of work a lot. My dad has told me that he swore he would never ever let that happen to his family. So, that's why he works so much, because he's afraid of being poor.

"A lot of times, I feel like ... well, Gene the group leader said not to say we 'feel like,' but instead to just state our feelings and accept responsibility for them. He says that when we use the word 'like' before our feelings we aren't fully accepting them or being responsible for them. So, I *feel* our relationship is poor. I feel disconnected from my dad because we don't spend much time together. Lately, he has been traveling even more because I believe it distracts him from the arguments that he and my mom always seem to be having. It appears that the worse things get at home, the harder he works."

I noticed that Jared didn't refer to his father as "my father" which is more impersonal. He continued to call him "my dad" which led me to believe that he still had a strong affection towards Stephen.

My interpretation was that Stephen Gantz was motivated by fear, fear of being poor. I had once heard that the actor Will Smith used fear to catalyze his motivation to achieve his dreams, specifically his fear of not achieving. While he was aware of the fear, he did not allow himself to get sucked into it. Instead, he saw what he didn't want, and then, as Ray had said months back, turned 180 degrees and refocused on what he *did* want. He used what he *didn't* want to catalyze his action to achieve what he did want. So Stephen's response to his childhood made sense.

"Hmm, whenever I've been over and both your folks are home, they seem to get along fine, but then I haven't seen your dad home much, so I guess I don't really have enough data to come to any accurate conclusions."

"Yes, my family believes in keeping its business to itself. From the outside, we are the model family. It's a different story once you get inside."

"I guess this has come up in the family session?"

"Well, yes, we've had two and I did share how I felt. My dad was rather quiet. I guess on some level he knew that it was true, but he didn't quite know how *much* I was affected by it. We have work to do."

"Yep, it's like anything else. Relationships are not necessarily good by default. They take work. Work in both the time you devote to them and the courage you bring to share your feelings. Many people are afraid of sharing their feelings because it means they're vulnerable. They see it as a weakness, but it's not. It's honest and it's real.

"In vulnerability lies the key to the strongest connections. There is always the chance you could feel hurt when you allow yourself to show up vulnerably but, on a much higher level, there is an opportunity to connect in a way that is simply impossible without letting your guard down. For any battle to be resolved, someone has to be the first to put down his sword."

"Hmm, I never considered it that way, but as I think back on yesterday's session, the thing that was best was that everyone in my family was being real. We cried, we spoke, my dad told me he understood, and it looked like he was really shook up. He seemed more real to me."

"Yes, when an event occurs in a person's life that it outside the set of default reactions or conditioned responses that that person has, he has to revert to his most primal, most basic human responses. He shows up in all of his humanness. That is a vulnerable response. You get to see that pure human reaction at funerals, births, and other emotionally charged events for which we have had no preparation.

"You admitting yourself to the hospital was an intelligent choice for you to keep yourself safe, AND it was an intelligent choice—although I'm sure it's not *why* you did it—to bring your family together for a bit of a reality check. By following what was true and right for you, it was also right for everyone else. Everyone gets to win."

He nodded in contemplation.

I let the silence of his thoughts fill the room. Jared didn't say anything. He just squinted his eyes a bit, a small smile formed on his face, and he nodded in understanding.

"Are you going to be able to keep up with your school work?"

"Well, all of my college applications were submitted in January and this week we're actually on break. I have a project due when we get back, but most of my research on it is done. So, I should be fine."

"I have some time on Thursday to come by. I don't start teaching until 1:30. Can I come by around noon?"

"Sure, noon on Thursday is great. Thanks for coming by tonight."

I got my coat and hat from the closet alcove and extended my hand which Jared reached for and then wrapped his other arm around my neck in a hug. When he hugged me, I noticed the book he was reading was *The Perks of Being a Wallflower*. It was tattered and dog-eared.

"See you on Thursday."

As I left the hospital, something about my interaction with Jared was gnawing at me. There was a disconnect for me between his words and my GUT. I sensed a bit of arrogance or unwarranted assuredness in him that I hadn't expected. I was expecting him to be broken. He felt strong and clear but in a textbook way. His answers felt canned and prepared, almost as though he was enjoying the attention he was getting. That concerned me, but I wasn't quite sure what to do about it or, even if I did know what to do, *if* I should do anything.

When I got home from the hospital, I noticed a message on my cell phone. The phone had never rung. When I checked it, it was from Stephen Ganzt.

"Hi, Matt. Jared told me you went to visit him tonight. Thanks for taking the time to see him. When you have a chance, would you give me a call? I'll be up until 10:00 tonight or, if that doesn't work, I'll be around in the morning before 11:00. Please call me on my cell." The time stamp on the message said the call was received at 9:30 PM, shortly after I had left the hospital.

I wrote Stephen's cell number on my message pad and looked at my watch. It was 9:45 PM and I hadn't eaten. I decided to have dinner and call Stephen in the morning. I'm sure that if it had been an emergency he would have said so on the message. Before I can be there for others, I have to be there for myself.

Flight attendants on airlines always tell you, "In the event of an emergency, secure *your* oxygen mask before helping others." The implication is that if *you* can't breathe you can't help others breathe. That makes sense. The first person in *your* life is *you*. A lot of people would see that as selfish, but it's not. I can't give what I don't have. If I don't make a deposit in the personal bank account called ME, I certainly can't withdraw from it. Investing in myself allows me to have something to give to others. So I decided that the rest of the night was mine.

I grabbed a yogurt from the fridge, mixed in some granola, and went to pour myself a glass of wine. Hmm, which wine goes well with yogurt? In a single guy's house, whichever one is open! It happened to be a merlot from the Napa Valley. I'm certain that the winemaker never intended to have his wine paired with Greek peach yogurt. One taste quickly confirmed my belief. I finished the yogurt, and I left the wine for dessert.

I was exhausted. Actually, a more accurate word was (one of Ray's self-titled Diamond Distinctions) *depleted*. My students were challenging and finishing up with Jared had drained me of whatever extra energy I might have had left. Listening, truly listening, requires a great deal of attention. The quiet of my home was about all the sound I could tolerate for the evening. I didn't even call Diane to say goodnight. After my second glass of wine, I changed for bed and set my alarm for 7:30 AM.

Seven thirty came around way too quickly. I was certain that when my alarm went off, I had only been sleeping a couple of hours. The weather did nothing to encourage me to get out of bed. It was gray and wet snow was falling, so I hit the snooze button and went back to sleep.

When I awoke, it was because the news on the radio had looped through, and I felt like I was in the movie *Groundhog Day*. I looked at my clock and the digital read out showed that I had overslept for exactly two hours and twenty-six minutes. It was 9:56 AM. Wow! I hadn't done that in a while! I guess my body was more depleted than I had realized.

When I got up, I noticed a text on my cell phone from Stephen Gantz. "Matt, my 11:00 AM meeting got moved up, and I'm only available until 10:00 AM. Please get to me before then. Thanks."

It was easy to tell when an older person was texting because there were no short cuts or abbreviations in the text. My student's texts ensured that the art of spelling would either be left to spell checks (when they were activated) or our language would deteriorate into a monosyllabic unpronounceable collection of acronyms. Speed was paramount. If only their fingers would move as quickly as their thumbs! They would all be concert pianists!

I had missed Stephen's 10:00 AM text by fifteen minutes. I decided to text him back anyway, as I was beginning to get concerned, having heard from him twice in twelve hours.

"Sorry I missed ur" backspace delete, delete, I guess my students were rubbing off on me! "your call. Will reach out to you at 11:30. Hope all is okay." I set a reminder on my cell for 11:25 so I didn't miss the appointment.

My morning consisted of designing worksheets, playing through a new piece to see if it was suitable for a student who was going into a competition and catching up with Diane. I called her at 10:45.

The phone rang once and she picked up.

"Hi, Matt."

"Hi, beautiful! How are you?"

"I'm good, disappointed that the weather was too nasty to go out for a run, but overall, good. How are you?"

"Good, but I was tired! I didn't get out of bed until after ten."

"Wow, that's late for you. How did things go with your student in the hospital? Did you visit him last night?"

"Yes, I did. I'm not really sure. It was a bit weird. I left feeling a disconnect between my GUT and what he shared with me. I'm not quite sure why. His dad left me a message on my cell around 9:30 last night, but I haven't connected with him yet."

"What was your GUT telling you? You know it's always right."

"That's just it, I don't know. I felt like he was too 'okay' with the situation. I expected him to look broken, but he actually looked and sounded great, well not great, but at least much better than I expected. It just didn't make sense. I mean when I arrived, he looked like he was just relaxing reading a book."

"What was he reading?"

"I don't know, something about perks or flowers or something."

"*The Perks of Being a Wallflower?*"

"Yeah, that was it. Why?"

"You've obviously never read the book or seen the movie. Charlie, the fifteen-year-old main character is admitted to a mental hospital after a series of coming-of-age events."

"Can you get more specific about the coming-of-age events?"

"Well, there was a realization that he had been sexually abused by an aunt when he was younger, a friendship with a guy who was gay and dating a football player, first love stuff, and truth or dare—standard twenty-first century coming-of-age stuff. Think of it as the twenty-first century *Catcher in the Rye*."

Hmm, I found that odd. On one hand, Jared was speaking about focusing on what he wanted and then on the other, the reading he was doing seemed to be more supportive of what caused him to admit himself to the hospital in the first place. This new information started to provide evidence that my GUT may not have been too far off. Good to know that my instincts were still on, disconcerting to believe that there might be "trouble in River City."

"I'm going to reach out to his dad around 11:30 AM and see what he wanted."

"Are you available for lunch today?" Diane asked.

"I wish I could, but with students off from school, I start teaching at 1:00 PM and go straight through until 9:00 PM."

"Okay. I'll miss you. Maybe we can catch up tonight?"

"That'll be great."

"Good luck with your student's dad."

"Thanks. Talk with you later."

At 11:30, my cell rang. It was Stephen.

"Hello?"

"Hi Matt, it's Stephen Gantz. Is this a good time to chat for a few minutes?"

"Sure, this works. What's on your mind?"

"Jared told me you visited him last night. Thank you, again."

"You're welcome."

"I'm not really sure what he shared with you, but the doctor called us yesterday to let us know that they're keeping him for further observation for the next several days. What kind of mood was he in when you saw him?"

"He looked good. He was telling me about the meetings with the counselor, why he admitted himself, and some of the things on his mind."

"Matt, the reason the doctor is keeping him for further observation is because they want to test him for bi-polar disorder. I believe it used to be called manic-depressive disorder."

Bi-polar disorder? That would explain my disconnect.

"That sort of connects some of the dots for me, Stephen."

"You mean because he 'looked good' to you?"

"Yes. I left with a gnawing feeling that he was projecting a way too stable and healthy image than I would've expected considering what he shared with me on the phone."

"Well, the doctors have put him on lithium and, while it usually takes up to several weeks for it to kick in, maybe there's a placebo effect for him, along with the fact that he's getting a lot of attention from the family."

"I understand. He mentioned that the family was also in counseling."

There was silence on the phone as I sensed that Stephen was considering the impact of my last statement.

"Matt, I'm sure that Jared is sharing things with you that give you insight into my family that most are not privy to. I can only request that the information he shares with you remain only with you. We, well, I did the best I could do in raising a son. Jared came along at a time in my life when my business was starting to take off. So, I'm sure that some of his issues and problems can easily be traced back to my absence and inattentiveness in his formative years."

I paused before responding, feeling both compassion and understanding. I was clearly wearing my teacher hat.

"Stephen, first, let me assure you, as I've shared with Jared, that anything he shares with me, unless it is something that I feel will lead to physical or emotional trauma for him, will remain confidential. While I understand you might also be feeling stressed ...." I really wanted to use the word *guilty,* but I thought it might offend him, "I am very certain that, at the time you made your choices you always made what you believed to be the best choice with regard to your business and your family. Looking back with different data, you can certainly scorn those choices, but at the time you made them, you saw them as your best options."

"You're very kind," Stephen replied.

"I'm not necessarily trying to be kind. I truly believe what I just said."

"Really?"

"Yes, I don't say what I don't mean just for the sake of saying something."

"I never quite thought about it that way. I guess it's similar to how I run my business. I'm given data to evaluate, and then I have to make the best decision based upon that data. If new data arrives which contradicts my decision, it doesn't mean my initial decision was bad, it just means that, with the new data, there's another decision to make. It's very objective, non-judgmental thinking. Hmm, I never quite saw it that way with my family. I just felt ... well, guilty and neglectful as I looked back on some of my decisions. I labeled them as bad decisions."

"I can see how you could feel that way. Do you really believe that at the time you made those decisions you were making bad decisions?"

"Well, when you put it that way, it would be crazy for me to say 'Yes.'"

"The question now is do you want to continue feeling guilty, or do you want to make decisions that will bring you and your family to a different place than you're presently at?"

"Now I see why Jared enjoys working with you. You cut right to the point, but not in an abrasive way. You see things very clearly. Have you ever considered a job in a more corporate environment?"

He hadn't answered the question. I waited. Silence creates a vacuum. Vacuums need to be filled. Stephen met this need.

"You certainly appear to have the skill set of a good manager."

Even as his son was in crisis, Stephen continued to be on the lookout for ways to build his company.

"You know what Stephen, what's most important now, is Jared and your family. If, in the future, such an opportunity exists, we can talk further." I offered, both as a humble way to leave his offer open and not insult him, but more to refocus him on what was presently the priority.

"That works. I originally thought the purpose of my call was to make you aware of the potential for Jared to be diagnosed as bi-polar. Apparently, the real purpose of my call was for you to help me refocus my attention in a more productive manner. Thank you."

"You're welcome."

CHAPTER 17

I received a call from Ray on Wednesday morning. It had been NOTES: two weeks since we had last seen each other as our schedules were polar opposites.

"Hi Matt."

"Hi Ray, how are things going? You ready for a concert at Carnegie Hall?" I teased.

"Sure, as long as I'm in the audience and not on the stage!" Ray replied quickly.

"How is your piano playing going? Did you call to set up another lesson?" I asked.

"I'm enjoying being a student. The going is slow by my expectation, but I'm enjoying the process and feel like I'm moving forward," he said.

"Great. So, do you want to get another lesson in?" I asked.

"Sure, but there's not a lot to show you. How about we have a lunch with an appetizer of a piano lesson?" he responded.

"Lunch sounds good. There's been a lot of stuff going on for me lately and I'd love to share it with you. I'm off on Friday, or I could also do Saturday afternoon," I offered.

"Friday sounds good. Your house at noon?"

"That works. See you on Friday."

LESSONS WITH MATT

I had moved my Friday lessons to Wednesday and Thursday so Diane and I could see a concert on Friday night. Today, I had eight straight hours of teaching ahead of me. I packed some healthy snacks (yogurt, two pieces of fruit, a granola bar, and a large bottle of water), and I left for my first lesson at 12:30.

When I finished teaching around 9:00, I had contemplated stopping for a couple of slices at that cell-phone-free pizzeria, but decided I just wanted to get home.

Upon arrival, I found a note from Diane. "Missed you today. I passed by around 8:00 and put a container of homemade chicken soup in the fridge so you wouldn't resort to pizza. I also left some homemade cookies on the counter. They'll go great with a cup of espresso (decaf!). Give me a call once you settle in. Love ya." She knew me so well.

What a welcome surprise. After a full day of teaching, I was famished as well as mentally and physically spent. The chicken soup was just what the doctor ordered!

I heated it up, cooked some pasta to put in the soup, and poured myself a generous glass of white wine. After the soup, I moved on to dessert. The cookies she had left were tantalizing. I tried to eat just one, but I finished the entire stack of eight! Life was good.

After I had eaten and cleaned up, I called her.

"Thanks for the soup it was great! Just what I needed after a cold day on the road. Certainly better than a carb-filled pizza!

"Those cookies were awesome too! What were they? Cinnamon? Molasses? You were right. They worked perfectly with a cup of espresso."

"Oh, they're just a recipe I've been playing around with lately. I don't really have a name for them yet."

"Well, put a name on them and sell them! They're fantastic!"

We spoke about our days, tossed around the idea of getting together and then decided to nix it because neither of us wanted to leave the warmth of our homes. We contemplated meeting for lunch tomorrow, but when we compared our teaching schedules, they just didn't line up. She was out west, and I was out east. She started her day at 9:00 AM and finished by 5:00; I started my day at 1:30 PM and finished at 9:30. We decided to just meet up on Friday night.

Thursday came and, after handling some morning business, I went to visit Jared at the hospital. When I arrived, he was just coming out of his group and shuffling towards his room from the opposite direction. He was wearing a bathrobe and slippers. It appeared he hadn't taken much care with shaving or fixing his hair, and he seemed to be agitated.

As we got closer, I gently called out to him.

"Hi, Jared."

He looked at me a bit confused and then said, "Hi, Matt. What are you doing here?"

"When I was here on Tuesday, I said I would come visit today at noon."

"Oh, I forgot."

"Would you prefer that I left?"

"Nah, I guess you can stay. It's been a tough morning. I just talked with my group for an hour."

"Okay, we can just sit in your room if that works for you."

"Sure, whatever."

He lumbered into the room and collapsed onto the bed, both from the earth's gravity as well as what appeared to be the gravity of whatever was weighing on his mind.

LESSONS WITH MATT

I removed my coat, hung it up in the closet, and took a seat next to the bed against the wall.

Jared stared at the ceiling's acoustical tiles in silence.

I could hear the ticking of the clock on the wall as well as people walking in the hallway. Jared turned over on his right side, his back to me and lifted his knees into a fetal position. I heard him take a deep inhale and then let out a short grunt that turned into a sigh.

"They took my book away."

I didn't know how to respond, so I said nothing.

"It was a gift from a friend."

Apparently, his words didn't yet require a response.

"They said it wasn't appropriate reading for someone in my condition."

"I liked it, though."

Jared rolled over onto his left side and faced me. He slowly sat up, lowering his feet over the edge of the bed and onto the floor. He reached up and thoroughly scratched his head, making even more of a mess of an already bad hair day.

I attempted a joke, "Bad hair day?"

He shrugged his shoulders, "Bad day."

I nodded my head in understanding.

"The doctors are running tests to see if I'm bi-polar."

"Has the doctor prescribed any meds for you?" I asked.

"Yes. They're not even sure they're the right meds for me. I guess that's why they say doctors *practice* medicine. They're practicing on me!"

In defense of his doctors, I replied, "Everyone is different. They've never met a Jared Gantz before. They have no way of knowing how you will respond."

"Yeah, I guess."

"So, what do you want?"

"I don't know."

"If you did know, what would it be?"

I waited.

"I want to be normal. No, that's not it. I just want to feel happy and at peace. I always thought my contrasting moods were because I was a creative Gemini, but now I'm finding out I may be bi-polar. I don't want to be bi-polar. I HATE that label, that title! I don't want it! I want my book!

"I don't want to be on meds. That's not normal. I don't want to be confused about my sexuality. I don't want to decide which college I'm going to! I don't want to do anything! I just want people to leave me alone and give me back my damned book!"

In a quieter voice, with his head down between his legs, he began to sob and continued, "I just want to be loved and accepted for whomever I am whenever I am it." I let this statement float around the room for a bit. It felt foundational to his mood. It felt authentic.

"I can see how frustrated you are. I get it." I paused to see if he was going to continue. After a good minute, I continued.

"Did you ever consider playing with the idea that *you* are not bi-polar but instead have a bi-polar disorder? Like people who have multiple sclerosis aren't MS. The have MS. You have a bi-polar disorder. People who have MS are managed and treated for MS. That's what doctors do. People with bi-polar, get treated for bi-polar. That's what doctors do. You don't have to label yourself as the disease or disorder."

"Yeah, I guess,"

I sensed the door wasn't open for incoming information so I refrained from offering any more. I would just be serving myself. I simply sat with him in silence; sometimes silence is the only thing that can fill the space.

At 1:00, I got up and left; Jared had fallen asleep on the bed.

CHAPTER 18

Friday morning arrived and it felt good to have a day off. While I was enjoying teaching infinitely more since I had readjusted my mission and approach, I had been looking forward to some down time.

The main difference in my approach was that I was more consistently aware of what I wanted and how it aligned with my mission. My mission was very simple—to provide the optimum learning environment in which my student could create feelings of success at the piano, while simultaneously creating this environment with the least amount of stress to myself.

This awareness allowed me to make better choices, choices that permitted me the opportunity to respond, instead of simply react. Throughout my day, I would ask myself, "Matt, what do you want?" Sometimes, I'd even say it out loud! Yet, life, like music, was made up of both sound and silence and today was a day of silence. The only things on my agenda were lunch with Ray and the evening concert with Diane.

I started the day with a run. The weather was crisp and still cold, but once I finished the first mile or so, I was warm enough to remove my gloves. I had decided to run for time, not distance. My goal was one hour and fifteen minutes. I had also decided not to run on one of my typical routes. I just wanted to let my mind wander, see new things, and run for the joy of running.

After the run, I did some strength exercises, stretched out for a half hour, and then took a long hot shower. I had bought a new "old school" safety razor, so I was excited about shaving with it. Most men saw shaving as a chore. For me, it was a meditation—the moistening of my skin, the lathering of the shaving cream on the brush, the scrape of the razor across my skin. Anything that created a presence or oneness of mind was a meditation.

For me, meditating was not just about sitting in a cross-legged position counting my breaths or saying a mantra all with the intent of clearing my mind. I found that almost impossible! Once you've realized you've cleared your mind, it's no longer clear! To me, meditation is about acceptance. It's about presence. Nothing saps us of energy more than multi-tasking. I know it's the rave of the business world—the ability to simultaneously eat; conduct a meeting; and answer phone calls, emails, and texts. Just the thought of it gives me a headache. A person's entire day could be a giant ongoing meditation if they could just learn how to be in the moment, like a child.

Children live in the moment. Children are in a constant meditative state because they exist solely with whatever it is they're doing. This is a wonderful thing! Parents are adults who have, either fortunately or unfortunately (depending upon your perspective), learned how to *not* live in the moment. As adults, we're conscious of how much time is *left* in a day.

I often hear parents telling me that they don't want to force their child to practice the piano. Learning to play the piano is work and requires time. The work is the road that connects a person's dreams to their reality. While I do agree that it is not prudent to drag a child by the ear to the piano, with that said, children, because they *do* live in the moment, do not have the necessary skills to manage their time effectively. The only time for a child is *now*. They exist solely for the present moment and unless that present moment is playing the piano, it's not necessarily good for learning the piano. That's where a parent comes in.

Parents need to assist their child in managing his or her time so that the child has scheduled piano playing/learning time. We do not have a genetic disposition for time management. It is a skill and, like all other skills, learnable. Children need to be *taught* this skill.

I completed my shaving meditation with a splash of aftershave and got ready for the rest of my day.

A few minutes before noon, my doorbell rang. As expected, Ray was right on time for his lesson.

"Good afternoon, Ray. Great to see you," I said, welcoming him in.

"Hi, Matt. Did you run this morning?" He didn't wait for me to reply. Instead, he continued enthusiastically, "It was a great morning, a little cold at the start, but invigorating. I even broke out the shorts today."

"Yes, I did, I went out for a fun run. No speed goals. I just wanted to keep moving for an hour and fifteen. It really cleared my head."

"Stuff on your mind?" Ray asked.

"Ray, you know me, there's *always* stuff on my mind, but we can get into it later. How about a cup of espresso?"

"That sounds good. Thanks."

I ground the beans, tamped exactly 19.5 grams into the porta filter, and loaded it into the espresso machine. While the shot dripped, I reached into my cabinet and placed a small, sweet biscotti on the saucer to provide a balancing element to the bitterness of the espresso. Life, music, and even coffee were about balance.

So much of life's gifts were in the contrasts. Music was all about contrasts: high and low, loud and quiet, fast and slow, melody and harmony, consonance and dissonance, tensions and resolutions. The tension moves the music forward until the listener experiences the resolution. Ravel's *Bolero* was a wonderful experiment of how long a build of tension could continue. Much of life's magic was in the contrast. Contrast provides balance.

The shot finished in twenty-seven seconds and had a nice crema. Perfect.

Ray drank the shot as they do in Italy, one tip of the small cup and the beverage was gone.

"Another?" I asked

"No, that was just right," Ray responded.

As with any good cup of espresso, there was a nice residue of crema in the cup. In France, they rinse the cup with Anisette, a sweet licorice-tasting liqueur. In the spirit of France, I offered Ray a bit of Anisette. He politely declined. After all, it was just noon.

"So how is your piano playing coming? When we spoke on the phone, you mentioned it was slow but enjoyable. That's good," I said.

"It's good that it's slow?" Ray asked.

"Sure. What's the rush? You don't have an up-coming concert that you have to perform in, do you?" I asked with sarcasm.

"No, but if it's slow, am I practicing enough?" Ray asked.

"Are you enjoying the process of playing and learning the piano?"

"Yes."

"Would playing more bring you greater enjoyment?" I asked.

"Getting better a bit faster would probably make playing more enjoyable," Ray replied.

"Ray, you played baseball professionally. Can the learning process for becoming a good batter happen faster or does it just take a certain amount of time or a certain number of swings to become a good hitter?"

"Yes, it's just about accurate repetition. As a matter of fact, I recently read somewhere that it takes 10,000 hours of focused practice to become a master at something. So I guess I only have about 9,990 hours left at the piano!"

I laughed and replied, "You'll learn how to play, of that I'm sure. But what is most important is that you learn accurately when you start. Just as with anything in life, speed is the result of accurate and comfortable practice."

"What do you mean comfort?" Ray asked.

"Well, like I say to my younger students, who always want to play fast and usually before they're ready to do so, when you first learned to ride a bike did you immediately try to go really fast?"

"No."

"What did you do?"

"I just tried to not fall off," he responded.

"Right, you tried to be safe. You wanted to feel comfortable. Then, as you started to feel more confident and comfortable with maintaining your balance, did someone have to convince you or force you to go faster, or did you just do it because you simply knew you could?"

"I did it simply because I wanted to and because it was fun," Ray replied.

"Learning the piano is the same process. You *will* be able to play faster if you practice whatever you're learning by playing slowly and accurately. The speed will simply happen as a result of *comfort*. You won't be able to prevent it from getting faster!

You will actually have to pay attention to keep a more consistent tempo that does not get away from you."

"That sounds like great fun, knowing a piece so well that my fingers just go on their own. I get it, so I guess I should just be more patient," Ray replied.

"Sure, if that's what it takes for you to continue to enjoy playing and learning the piano.

"Would you like to play something?" I asked.

"No, I believe our lesson is complete. It's exactly what I needed, a bite size piece of useable inspiration. I just need to play more and exhibit a bit of patience with myself. Are you ready to go to lunch?"

"Sure. There's a new restaurant in town that just opened, and I heard it has a large selection of craft beers and great specialty burgers. How's that sound?"

"Sure, I could go for a good burger. I'll drive," Ray replied.

Ray pressed the button on his remote to unlock his blue Jeep Wrangler (if my ears were serving me correctly I believe the pitch of the chirp was a B flat). Before I got in, he reached over to the passenger side of the car and moved a tattered Bible and a bunch of travel brochures to the back seat. I saw brochures describing scuba tours of Cocos Island, Costa Rica, Red Sea, Egypt, and one for Nouméa, New Caledonia.

Cars are very personal spaces. You can learn a lot about someone from just being a passenger in his or her car. The music they listen to, if they are neat or sloppy, what they read, if they have an animal, if they're involved in sports, even what scents they like!

"Taking another trip sometime soon?"

"Considering it. I've always wanted to go scuba diving off the Great Barrier Reef, that's the one that seems the most promising at the moment."

"You're scuba certified?"

"Yes, I've been diving since I was a kid."

"I'm a landlubber. Breathing underwater makes no sense to me. I once tried scuba while on vacation in Florida. The resort had an instructor come in and give lessons in the pool. As soon as I tried to take my first breath underwater, I panicked. It was contrary to everything I understood about breathing. In martial arts and meditation, for the most part conscious breathing occurs *in* through the nose and *out* through the mouth. Scuba breathing was exactly the opposite of this, and I felt like I had to think about the most essential involuntary process to keep myself alive! I couldn't get past the anxiety, so I never tried again."

"I can see how that could cause you anxiety. I guess I was young enough when I started that I just never thought about it. For me, there is something so freeing about floating around the ocean surrounded by sea life. I love it."

Besides the brochures and the Bible, Ray's car was extraordinarily neat. There was a CD player in the dashboard and some Elvis hair on the back seat. The console between the driver and passenger's seats was filled with coins, some were American, and others appeared to be foreign currency.

"Does Elvis like to go for rides?" I asked.

"When the weather is nice, I take the top off and Elvis is in heaven. He just sits in the back with his nose pointed straight up in the air, catching every little scent that passes. I can only imagine what he smells!"

"Do you read the Bible every day?" I asked.

"Yep. It has some pretty neat stories." Ray replied.

"So, you're Christian?" I continued.

"I guess you could say that. I don't really go to church, but I do like the concepts in the Bible. Most of the stuff you and I have spoken about can be found in the Bible in one way, shape, or form."

The restaurant was just three miles away; it was owned and run by a husband and wife team. From the article in the local newspaper, the husband, Will, was a retired Wall Street trader who was also an amateur chef and his wife, Winnie, had gone to culinary school. They named the restaurant WW1. I wonder if they had any intentions of opening WW2 or starting WW3 someday?!

The hostess brought us to a booth in the back and placed our menus on the table. "Your server will be Darma, and she'll be right over to take your drink orders," the hostess said cheerfully.

Fully aware of my discomfort with having my back to the door, Ray waited for me to sit in the seat that was most comfortable for me. As expected, I chose the one that permitted me to keep my back to the wall, so I could face the entrance and the rest of the restaurant.

"Thanks," I said.

"You're welcome," Ray replied with a knowing smile.

As I reviewed the beer menu, I noticed the place had a full lunch crowd for a Friday, probably because of the article that had appeared in this past Tuesday's newspaper. The reviewer described the signature stuffed burger as "One of the best stuffed burgers I've ever had! It's made with the freshest organically raised beef, ground every morning by Chef Will, stuffed with chorizo sausage and Havarti cheese, and topped with sautéed shiitake mushrooms. The contents are hugged by a lightly toasted brioche bun that creates the perfect bun to meat ratio." I knew what I was having.

Darma came over, introduced herself, and asked if she could take our drink orders.

"I'll have a pint of Curieux, please."

Curieux was a beer from Maine that sits in bourbon barrels for a couple of months. It takes on a distinct but soft vanilla flavor from the barrels.

"And for you, sir?" Darma asked as she turned to Ray.

"I'll have a glass of club soda with a lime, please."

"I'll be right back with your drinks," Darma stated as she left.

"Too early for a beer?" I asked Ray.

"Yep," Ray replied.

"Well it's 5:00 somewhere!" I said.

"So, what's on your mind, Matt?" Ray asked.

"What do you mean?" I replied. I hadn't remembered saying anything that would motivate his question.

"When I arrived at your house you said that there was a lot going on. I was just following up on your comment."

"Oh, yes. I just wasn't in that mode when you asked me the question. I was still considering the beer. Hmm, where to start? Well, I guess the biggest thing is with one of my high school students."

Ray maintained eye contact with me and waited. Silence creates a vacuum that, like all vacuums, eventually desires to be filled.

"The short of it was that on Monday, I got a call from the father of one of my students. He called to let me know that the student had admitted himself to a hospital because he was afraid he was going to hurt himself," I said, filling the vacuum.

"Why did the student's father call you?" Ray asked.

"Because the student was permitted to list ten people who were allowed to visit him. The list had the name of his immediate family members, an aunt, an uncle, and me."

"Hmm," was Ray's reply, as he appeared to consider the implications of the call.

Darma arrived with our drinks and asked us what we wanted for lunch.

"I'll take the signature WW1 burger, medium rare, please."

She turned to Ray. "I'll have the same, but medium, please."

Darma left and I was in the middle of swallowing my first sip of the beer when Ray said, "I guess you have to be careful what you wish for."

"What do you mean?" I asked.

"Do you remember last year when you were at my home, and I asked you what you wanted?"

"Sure, how could I forget? At first I thought you were asking me what I wanted in my coffee only to find out that you were asking me the more existential question of what I wanted in my life."

"Yes, and do you remember your reply?"

"Yes. It was something about influencing my students beyond their piano skills."

"I remember your response very well. You said that you wanted to know that you were having a lifelong impact on your students. Be careful what you wish for," Ray replied with a raised eyebrow.

He was right. I did ask for that and now, in the most unsuspecting ways, I was receiving it.

"It reminds me of a quote from one of Franklin Delano Roosevelt's speeches, which he actually never gave, having died between the time the speech was written and the day he was supposed to have delivered it," I said.

"Do you mean 'With great power comes great responsibility'?" Ray asked.

"Yes, that's it," I replied.

"Well, many people attribute that quote to Spiderman's grandfather, Ben. I believe, however, Voltaire was the first one to make the reference," Ray continued.

"I felt humbled by the fact that I was put on the student's list of trusted persons, but I'm not a therapist or a psychologist. I'm just a piano teacher."

"Oh no, you can't do that," Ray gently chastised.

"Do what?"

"Back off to being *just the piano teacher*. That's not what you asked for. That was not your vision. You have received exactly what you asked for. Now accept the responsibility that comes with the granting of that wish."

I knew he was right. "Fair enough," I replied.

Darma arrived with our food. The burgers looked perfect—a beautiful char around the edges, shiitake mushrooms attempting to escape from beneath the bun, and the correct amount of messiness to be inviting. I picked it up firmly and gripped it with both hands, elbows out so the anticipated juices wouldn't drip down my arms. I took a healthy bite and was not disappointed.

The burger was a perfect medium rare and was accompanied by double batter dipped thick-cut fries. The Havarti cheese and chorizo that was stuffed into the middle oozed out as I pulled the sandwich away from my mouth. "Mmmm, this is superb," I said through a mouthful of burger.

Ray was still biting into his burger, so he just nodded his head in approval.

"That is some burger," I said again as I washed it down with a sip of the Curieux.

"You really get excited about food," Ray stated.

"I guess I do. Coffee, food, wine, beer. I guess you could say I have an oral fixation. I'm sure a Freudian psychologist would have a field day with me. But you have to admit, that is some burger," I said with a chuckle.

"I don't have to admit it, but I will. It's an excellent burger. Good choice of restaurant."

Continuing where we left off, Ray stated, "So how is your student doing? Have you gone to see him?"

"Yes. I visited him twice. Once on Tuesday evening after I finished teaching and then again yesterday afternoon before I started teaching. Generally, he seems okay."

"Generally?" Ray asked quizzically.

"Well, yes. I won't say he's good. Heck, he admitted himself to a hospital. But I guess, overall, he's okay. To be candid, our conversation felt a bit awkward. It was real but a bit, I don't know, strained."

"Do you think the strain you felt was your own discomfort?"

"Yes, that could be it. I've never had this kind of situation in my life before, so it was new," I replied.

"So, is the young man going home soon?"

"I'm not really sure. He was being tested for bi-polar disorder when I spoke with him yesterday. I don't know how long they'll keep him once he's diagnosed," I replied.

"I guess he just has to take it one day at a time," I continued.

As we finished our last bites of our burgers, Darma came over and asked if we needed anything else.

"I'm fine," Ray replied appearing to have his thoughts interrupted when she asked her question.

"I'm fine also. We'll just take a check."

"Lunch is on me," I said.

"Let's split it," Ray replied.

"No, it's on me," I held firmly.

"Okay, then let me leave the tip," Ray countered.

"No, like I said, it's on me," I repeated.

"Why are you being so stubborn?" Ray challenged.

"Why can't you just be gracious and say 'Thank you'?" I asked.

Ray considered my statement and replied, "Thank you."

"You're welcome."

Many people find it difficult being good receivers. Receiving and giving are just different sides to the same coin. Being a good receiver allows your "receiver bucket" to fill so that it overflows and you can then be a great giver. You can't give what you don't have.

We walked out to Ray's car and the double B flat chirp of his alarm signaled that it was okay to try the handles on the door.

When we got in the car, Ray was quiet and a bit distant. I asked him if everything was okay, figuring that the interaction over the bill had him thinking.

"Yes," he said as he reached into his console for some change.

"You know, Matt, you're one hundred percent right, but not just for your student, for all of us. We only get life one day at a time, so we can only live life one day at a time. Sometimes it's one minute at a time. That philosophy is what has gotten me here today."

He looked down into his palm;.he was holding a coin from a foreign country.

"Matt, I'm a recovering alcoholic. I just celebrated my thirtieth year of sobriety," he said as he exposed his anonymity and the coin in his hand. It was an Alcoholics Anonymous thirty-year medallion. I recognized it because two of my college buddies had respectively just celebrated their tenth and fifteenth years of sober living.

I had spent many hours listening to them speak about their alcoholism and the AA program. I had watched them get on and fall off "the wagon." So I was aware of some of the general challenges Ray had been through and the incredible accomplishment it was to remain sober for thirty years. With this new information, so much clicked into place for me. Why he had turned down the Anisette, why he ordered club soda and lime, why the Bible was tattered. He probably carried it every place he went. I felt a bit uncomfortable having exposed him to the alcohol, but realized, from my two college buddies, that that was his life, not mine. So much more about him made sense.

"When is your anniversary?" I asked.

"Yesterday, March 4th, which is both a date and a mantra for me."

CHAPTER 19

I visited Jared once more on Monday. His mood appeared to be level and more authentic. He had reticently let me know that he had, in fact, been diagnosed with bi-polar disorder.

NOTES:

Jared's father called me on Tuesday afternoon.

"Hi Matt, it's Stephen. Jared is coming home tomorrow. We're having a family dinner around 6:00. Are you available to join us? You've become family in the past two weeks."

"Stephen, thanks for the offer, but I'm working until 8:30 on Wednesday. But, I'll come by over the weekend."

"Matt, Jared said he would still like to continue piano lessons with you. Do you have a spot for him in your schedule?"

"Sure, Stephen. I'll find time for him. Just a question, though. Is Jared sure he wants to study piano or does he just want to get together with me?"

"Good question and, to be honest with you, I don't have an answer. Regardless, I will gladly pay your tuition. You bring so much more into his life than just music."

"That's fine. I just wanted to make sure we're on the same page. You hired me to teach your son piano. I'm not a therapist or counselor or any other title requiring a license to be a mental health professional."

"I understand."

"I can put him on my schedule on Tuesday evenings at 8:00. He'll be my last stop of the night."

"Great. If you can find the time, we'd love to see you this weekend."

"Sure I'll designate the time. I'll give you a call to firm up a time I can come by this weekend and, for sure, I'll see Jared next Tuesday, the 19th."

Many people think they have to *find the time* for the things in their life. Time is always there, clicking away. There's no reason to go and *find it*. Where would you look? For me, an important distinction is the willingness to give someone your time, which is the only real commodity any of us have. Sharing your time with someone is an investment for both people.

"Thanks, Matt."

"You're welcome."

CHAPTER 20

For a couple of hours on Saturday morning, I visited with Jared and his family. They acted exactly as I would've expected of a family whose son had just come out of a hospital for mental illness: awkward laughter and lightness all with a gentle touch of cautious jubilance. While everyone was doing the best they could with the skills they had, the atmosphere was controlled optimism tinged with anxiety.

NOTES:

The following Tuesday, Jared and I met for a piano lesson. We chatted a bit about how his week was going, and then I asked him what he wanted to do.

"Like I've said before, I want to live a happy, clear life. I want to feel healthy. I don't want to feel afraid of my own thoughts. I want to be okay in my own skin." Jared responded quickly and defensively.

I laughed inside as he answered the question not in the manner I intended it. He reminded me of someone I knew very well. I let him finish and nodded my head. "Those are some wonderful goals. And when you shared them with me at the hospital, I heard you. What I was asking was about what you want to do at the piano today," I replied.

"Oh, my bad. Sorry," he replied sheepishly.

"No problem. Once again, it was good to hear you reiterate your goals. The more you focus on them, the quicker they will be yours. Your constant focus on your goals is part of the

169

consistent work you need to do in order to connect your dreams to your reality. Each piece of *work* is another paving stone in the path that moves your dreams into your reality."

"Hmmm, I never thought about *work* that way. It was always, well, work, something I had to do, usually reluctantly," Jared responded.

"Yes, most people have a negative connotation to the idea of work. 'I have to go to work today.' 'I can't meet you for dinner; I have to work.' 'Working for a living sucks.' The problem is that many people are not working on the correct thing. They call their way of earning a living *work*, but that's not the work I'm referring to.

"Your *work* is the only way of, as the saying goes, 'making your dreams come true.' When you get older, you may choose to do a job that earns you a living but has nothing to do with the work you need to do to connect your dreams to your reality. Then again, you might be one of the fortunate ones whose job is aligned with their dream and that's wonderful. You can make lists, create notes, and make a book with pictures of your goals all used to remind you of what you want but, without the *work*, those notes, lists, and books are still just reminders of the dream. The ONLY way to pull your dream into your reality is through work."

"But won't the lists and pictures keep me focused on what I want?"

"Absolutely. I'm not saying don't make a dream book or write those affirmations. They are valuable tools to assist you in achieving your dreams. What I *am* saying is that they are only one part of the strategic plan to achieve your dreams. Without action, i.e. work, the strategies of writing affirmations, praying, making beautiful goal books, will fail. You can meditate on what you want for as long as you want, but after you clear your mind and get a good image of your desires, you need to get up and take action. That's what you did when you admitted yourself to the hospital. You took action to get yourself closer to your goal of feeling healthy."

"Oh, I get it. Some of the work is in the decisions I make."

"Yes, decision making is part of the work. Your ability to make effective decisions is the only *true* power you possess. Life will happen; you will react or respond. If you react, your decision will mostly follow suit with all the other decisions you have made in your life, and you will literally be in the *circle of life*, basically going nowhere new. If, however, you create a miniscule *gap* between the happenings of your life and your *responses* to those happenings, you're creating the opportunity to get off the *carousel* of your life and onto the *path* of your life. Your life at any given point is the culmination of all of the decisions you have made up to that point. If you don't yet have what you want and you have been taking action, it is either because you just need to continue to take more of the same action or learn how to make better decisions which will thus create different actions."

"But, if I work really hard, shouldn't I ultimately get what I want?"

"Not necessarily. You can run east with all of your might, looking for a sunset, but you simply won't find one. Part of the work is being conscious of the results you're receiving. If you feel your work is getting you closer to your goal, then continue. If you don't see the goal coming closer, you might want to reassess and fine tune your decisions and thus your actions."

Jared paused a moment. The room was quiet with reflection.

"Can we work on learning how to compose so I can make my poems into songs?" he asked.

"Sure," I replied with a grin.

Our "piano" lessons continued over the next few months and Jared did actually put one of his poems to music. It was also good to hear that Jared and Stephen appeared to be talking more. When I arrived for Jared's piano lessons, I saw Stephen in the home a bit more often. I guess Jared's crisis intervention call intervened in many people's lives connected to Jared. We are all connected.

Come the end of May, Jared invited me to his high school graduation. I usually politely decline attending my student's events, trying to keep my business and personal relationships separated but, clearly, Jared's situation was different. He had also invited me to his graduation party, which was set for Saturday, June 26th, the day before his actual graduation ceremony. Jared and his family had planned a twenty-day vacation to Italy on Monday, the 28th, so they had arranged to have his graduation party before they left.

The party was an all-day event starting at 2:00 PM. Diane and I arrived shortly before 3:00. I was greeted with a warm welcome by his family and quickly found out that even his extended family knew my name, each of them exchanging glances of recognition as Stephen introduced me with his hand on my shoulder.

In the Gantz's impeccably manicured backyard, a tent, capable of accommodating 150 people, had been set up; it was unnecessary on this perfect seventy-eight-degree day.

Diane and I went to the buffet and filled our plates with some incredible barbequed ribs and pulled pork and then meandered around the party. I was surprised to find out that several of Jared's friends were also my students. They came over to me and gave me a very warm welcome. They each wore the same smile of infinite possibilities reserved for graduating high school seniors and anyone else who understood that the potential in their lives was ahead of them.

Diane leaned into me and placed a kiss on my cheek.

"What was that for?" I asked.

"I'm just proud that you're in my life," she said with a smile that lit up her entire face as well as my heart.

We were comfortable enough with each other that I was able to just receive her compliment without feeling the need to give her one back. That was one of the things that I loved about our relationship. There was no obligatory chatter. One "I love you" did not have to be followed by another. Sometimes it just felt good to hear those words without the compulsion to respond in a like manner. I found those three words to be extremely powerful and just let them sink into my being.

I wasn't certain what kind of gift I should bring Jared, so I gave him a check and a letter I had written him the night before. A year back, Ray's letter had made an incalculable impact in my life. Maybe, at the very least, my letter would inspire Jared in some small way. I wrote it on monogrammed ivory stationery I had received from a student this past December.

Jared,

It has been a great pleasure to work with you over the past years and watch you grow. You are a wonderful young student infinitely capable of achieving all you dream of.

As you continue on your path of life remember if you do not yet have what you want, please do not question your intelligence, your ability, your upbringing, or your environment but, instead, take a look at your commitment as demonstrated by your actions.

Certainly, it would be easier to blame your circumstances instead of your commitment. Many people would support you in such an empty venture for it also gives them an excuse for not pursuing their own dreams. "I don't have the right body type." "I wasn't born into the proper family." "I don't have the best social connections, the talent, the ability, or the intelligence." The list of excuses could go on! But NONE of that matters; all that matters is your desire and your ability to work.

Your dream becomes your wish once you think about it. Your wish becomes your goal once you write it down. Your goal becomes your commitment when you give it a deadline. Your commitment becomes your reality once you pave the road with bricks of your labor.

Many people create their lives from their circumstances. That's why many people continue to live their lives devoid of their dreams. They are the victims of their circumstances. This is simply not the most effective manner to create achievement! A victim is tied to the mast of the ship and only arrives in the ports chosen by others. If you choose, instead, to live your life from your commitment, you gain the control to sail your ship into the ports of your desires!

Commitment is your consistent pledge to achieve what you desire. The world responds with optimism and support to committed action. Commitment keeps you on course when distractions arise and you are tempted to avoid the work. Commitment is the blinder that a horse wears when surrounded by traffic so it is not spooked by the distractions around it.

Your potential is limitless. Athletes without the advantage of all of their limbs have gone on to achieve Olympic greatness simply because they refused to live their lives as victims. Great business owners have succeeded in spite of their attention deficit disorders, Turrets syndrome, ADHD, poor grades, and teachers and parents who told them they would amount to nothing. They succeeded simply because they refused to live their lives as victims! They *chose* to build their lives from their commitments, NOT their circumstances.

When all else is taken from you, you are left with one thing, your word. Multimillion-dollar contracts have been signed with a simple handshake, which was understood as a bond, a commitment of your word. The honor behind this handshake has long since been displaced by long-winded legal contracts that ultimately only benefit the people who were hired to compose them. Yet, in spite of this, to those who understand its full impact, the handshake continues to hold immeasurable value.

Who is the most important person to whom you *give your word?* No, it's not your best friend, significant other, or parent. Who is the most important person in your life? Yes ... you!

This is not to say that everyone else is any less important. That is simply not true. Everyone is important and everyone should have the highest priority of importance in their own lives. You need to be able to, above all else and everyone else, trust your commitment to yourself! Before you can ever extend your word to others, you must first be able to rely on it for yourself.

Certainly, you will have inner conversations about why you should not follow through on your commitment to yourself. "I'm tired." "I'm hungry." "I'm afraid." "I'm bored." "I wasn't born on the right side of town." "I didn't go to the best school!" This is the traffic that the horse is not permitted to see. Do not listen to the noise! Do not spend a second of your efforts looking for excuses of why you cannot achieve what you desire. Simply listen to what it is that you want and put all of your attention and efforts toward those goals.

Is this simple? Yes. Is it easy? No. Is it the only way for you to move your dreams from fantasy into reality? Yes.

Rest assured, you will stumble. You will lack in your commitment. What should you do when this occurs? Simply ask yourself, "What do I want?" and then recommit. The achievement of your life's dreams is not one long commitment; it is a series of continuous recommitments. There is no shame in recommitting.

The only power you have to achieve your goals is in your ability to work. You can only get closer to your dreams by working. Work is movement. Just as you cannot ski down a mountain without moving, you cannot bring your dreams into your reality without movement. Even if you find you are on a less than accurate path, you have only done so because you were in motion, working on achieving your goal. It is only in motion that you can turn. You cannot turn a car that is not moving, you cannot carve a curve into the snow with a ski that is not moving. Movement means you're working.

Certainly, just as when you're skiing, you continuously weave to avoid obstacles, you will also do so as you proceed to transfer your dreams into your reality. The path to your goals is a slalom. The turns are *part of the path*, not exceptions to it. There is no direct straight line to your dreams. All roads paved by work will be curved.

When you work, work with awareness. Be conscious of your results. Remember the runner who runs east with all of his being looking for a sunset. No one can fault him on his effort, except that it is futile simply because it is applied in the wrong direction. Take notice if your work is getting you closer to your goal. If it is not, simply and gently readjust your course appropriately.

"How do I readjust my course, when I don't know what to do?" Simple! Just do something else! That might sound strange, but to paraphrase a famous saying, "Doing something the same way over and over and expecting a different result is ... silly!" Do anything else and notice if you're getting closer to or further from your goal. If you're getting closer, continue doing more of the same until the results are again less than desired, and then simply readjust.

But you need to move! You need to work.

While it's important to keep a positive mental attitude, it alone will not assist you in achieving your desires. You must keep your eye on the prize you desire. Stay focused on what it is that you want to achieve. *What do you want?*

Your goals should entice you, not intimidate you. They should be inviting, not overwhelming, and certainly not boring. Be guided by the wisdom of Goldilocks and the Three Bears, not too large, not too small, just right.

I believe in you. I believe in your ability to work with enough of a focus to achieve all that you put your mind to. You can master a language, learn an instrument, ace a subject in school, make a sports team, ask someone on a date, say no to anything that puts you in harm's way, or build the next great Fortune 500 company.

Your ultimate reward for your work is the feelings of pride you create; these are the true fruits of your labors. A farmer can only harvest a crop on which he has worked. He plants, waters, fertilizes, and cares for the crop—all forms of work. His work culminates in harvesting the fruits of his labors.

When you were younger, the receipt of a trophy acknowledging your efforts was valuable. But think back, if you put no effort into that for which you were rewarded, wasn't your trophy a shallow victory? Was it a victory at all? I would think not. Your pride and feeling of accomplishment in your own being is certainly the greatest trophy of all and one you can carry with you everywhere you go.

Finally, remember, your feelings are not accidents. They are there to guide you. Your G.U.T. feeling, is your internal GPS. Your G.U.T. is, to quote a dear friend, "Guidance U Trust." The things you do that create feelings of pride and fulfillment are the things you should continue doing. The things that create embarrassment or any other feeling that is less than desirable are the things you should stop or avoid doing.

If you dream big enough, all of your dreams will come true ... GARBAGE! Most people forget about the most important part of the formula for turning your dreams into your reality! If you dream big enough and are willing to work hard enough, *then* all of your dreams will come true!

Your dreams are yours for the taking, but the taking is not free. The price is your labor, your work. Your life is about building the roadwork that brings your dreams into your reality. Do so with happiness, integrity, peace, and, above all, consistent kindness to yourself.

I'll leave you with a question. Tomorrow you will be one day older. Will you also be one brick closer in paving your road to the achievement of your dreams?

Your Friend,

Matt

The following day, at 10:00 AM, I went alone to Newfield High School; Diane had a family event. I sat in the bleachers with Jared's family; they had reserved a seat for me. Stephen gave me a big hug and was grinning from ear to ear. "There was a point this year when I was afraid I wasn't going to see this day," he said with tears in his eyes. I nodded my head in acknowledgement. He hugged me again.

I looked at the program listing the order of the graduation ceremony—speeches by the superintendent, the principal and the valedictorian, Jared Gantz! I had never realized he was first in his class, and he had never shared this information, not even at his party the day before. I always knew he was extremely bright (he was accepted to Princeton and had chosen to major in English with the intent of pursuing a master's degree in education), but I had never realized that he was the valedictorian of his class.

After the dignitaries gave their welcoming remarks, Jared got up to address his class. His speech was eloquent and concise. It lasted all of about two minutes and ended with the following lines:

"To paraphrase a letter I received from a friend, 'Always focus on what you want. Our dreams are ours for the taking, but the taking is not free. The price we pay is our work. With each piece of work we do, we put another stone in the road that connects our dreams to our realities. Dream big, work harder. Let's create our lives and our vision of the world, one paving stone at a time.'"

After his speech, his class rewarded him with a standing ovation. Later in the ceremonies, his school awarded him with the Josephine Mandino Scholarship for Education, which I later found out was given to one student in the county.

Fifteen minutes after the graduates threw their caps, Jared reunited with his family. As I was saying goodbye, he raised a folded ivory envelope with a monogrammed "M" in the upper left-hand corner. He smiled, nodded, placed the envelope in the right breast pocket of his suit, and extended his right hand for a handshake, which quickly became a hug.

The End

43374476R00117

Made in the USA
Lexington, KY
27 July 2015